THE DIGRESSIONS IN *BEOWULF*

MEDIUM ÆVUM MONOGRAPHS V

THE DIGRESSIONS IN *BEOWULF*

By ADRIEN BONJOUR

Chargé de cours à l'Université de Lausanne

BASIL BLACKWELL

OXFORD

1970

First printed 1950

Reprinted (photolitho) 1965, 1970

631 03370 x

PRINTED IN GREAT BRITAIN
FOR BASIL BLACKWELL & MOTT LTD.,
BY COMPTON PRINTING LTD., LONDON & AYLESBURY
AND BOUND BY
THE KEMP HALL BINDERY, OXFORD

To C. C. H.

WHOSE INTEREST IN THINGS
MEDIEVAL PROVED CONTAGIOUS

ACKNOWLEDGEMENTS

THIS paper was written in 1944 and its publication was delayed owing to war and post-war conditions. I am especially thankful to Dr. Onions, who suggested its inclusion in the Medium Ævum Monographs (but bears no responsibility for its form), and to Mr. Basil Blackwell, who was instrumental in seeing me through the practical and financial problems involved in the publication, in the present circumstances, of a highly (if not over) specialized study. Such problems, I am glad to say, lost much of their alarming character owing to generous grants from the Société Académique Vaudoise and the University of Lausanne.

Concerning the inception and the final form of the study, I owe the greatest debt to my master, Prof. G. A. Bonnard, who spared neither time nor efforts to supervise the text and offer invaluable suggestions. Prof. F. P. Magoun (who first introduced me to Anglo-Saxon at Harvard) and Prof. L. L. Schücking kindly sent offprints of articles inaccessible in what had become Island Switzerland in the sea of invaded Europe.

Finally, I express my gratitude to the many Beowulfian scholars cited in the notes, and particularly to three of the greatest, Prof. Fr. Klaeber, Prof. J. R. R. Tolkien, and the late Prof. R. W. Chambers.

AD. BONJOUR

VEVEY
December, 1949

CONTENTS

INTRODUCTION

I⊤ is perhaps no exaggeration to say that few other features are more characteristic of the *Beowulf* than the use of numerous digressions and episodes.[1] Though they represent less than a quarter of the poem, the investigations and comments to which they have given rise are probably as numerous as those which have been devoted to the rest of the poem.

As a matter of fact, the presence of such episodic matter in *Beowulf* created problems which have been abundantly discussed and are still in the foreground of *Beowulf* criticism.

At the dawn of such criticism, a little more than a century ago, scholars had already been struck by the composite character of the poem. They showed that the poem was composed, on the one hand, of a general narrative, which could be divided into three parts (i.e. the great fights of the hero), and, on the other hand, of a series of episodes which were but loosely connected with the main narrative.[2] Then, in the course of numerous studies and dissertations, this episodic material was submitted to closer and closer scrutiny, and the eight episodes originally distinguished by Ettmüller have now swelled into more than a score of digressional units in the elaborate lists of modern scholars.[3]

What does this episodic material actually consist in? As regards the form and presentation of the digressional units, two types may be distinguished: the episodes and the digressions. Strictly speaking, an episode may be considered as a moment which forms a real whole and yet is merged in the main narrative, whereas a digression is more of an adjunction and generally entails a sudden break in the narrative. As a genuine type of episode we have, of course, the Finnsburg Tale. Though its

---

[1] 'Routh has shown that *Beowulf* . . . has far more passages of the sort than any other Anglo-Saxon poems' (A. C. Bartlett, *The Larger Rhetorical Patterns in Anglo-Saxon Poetry*, New York, 1935, p. 86).

[2] R. Wülker, *Grundriss zur Geschichte der Angelsächsischen Litteratur*, Leipzig, 1885, p. 289.

[3] What should be regarded as episodic material or not in a poem like *Beowulf* is, of course, liable to variation, and depends largely on the critic's opinion. Variations do occur, in fact, if we compare the studies of Haeuschkel, Routh, Klaeber, and Bartlett; yet these variations are not considerable and the degree of agreement is quite satisfactory. For our part we have conformed to Professor Klaeber's classification which, on the whole, seemed to us most reasonable, and have generally adopted his own denominations of the different episodes. See F. Klaeber, *Beowulf and the Fight at Finnsburg*, 3rd ed., New York, 1936 (especially the section devoted to 'digressions and episodes', pp. liii-lv).

style is somewhat allusive, that part of the legend recited by the scop at the royal court is complete in itself; as a specimen of what the king's gleeman used to sing on such occasions, it is part of the description of the festivities in Heorot. As a type of digression we may cite the allusion to Modthrytho and Offa[1] (introduced with reference to the young Geatish queen), which rather abruptly interrupts the narration of Beowulf's return.

Needless to say such a distinction is not absolute. Some critics give the word 'episode' a very restricted sense whereas others use the terms 'episode' and 'digression' as synonyms.[2]

As regards their subject matter and length, on the other hand, the digressional units are of the greatest diversity. Events relating to early Danish history, to Geatish and Swedish history or to Germanic legends, as well as allusions to the hero's youthful adventures and references to Biblical passages, not to speak of moralizing or elegiac topics of a general character, all these form the substance from which the episodic matter has been drawn. In extent the digressional units 'range from cursory allusions of a few lines', such as the anticipation of the burning of Heorot, 'to complete and complicated narratives', such as the Finnsburg Tale or the Heathobard feud.[3]

Now if each individual digression has its own problems—and some of them are of great interest and variety—the one great question which is raised by the presence of so many and various digressions in the poem is that of their relation to the main story. The problem, which is of the highest importance as it is closely connected with the general problem of the composition and unity of the poem, is far from being solved. We

---

[1] *Beowulf*, 1931 ff.

[2] When speaking generally we shall use both terms indifferently: yet we shall apply the distinction when referring to an individual case and shall use the word 'episode' in accordance with our definition and whenever the term has been consecrated by tradition. We here endorse Professor Klaeber's remark that 'a rigid distinction between "digressions" and "episodes" as attempted by Smithson . . . who considers the accounts of Sigemund-Heremōd and the Finnsburg Tale the only episodes, need not be applied' (*ibid.*, p. liii).

We are quite aware, finally, that what might be called the episodic character of all the digressional passages listed by Klaeber presents a great diversity. Yet there is no need to take this character in so restricted a sense as Miss Bartlett, when she writes that 'of all the so-called episodic material, only the Finn lay can be said to be a real digression from the principal narrative; and it, of course, is by no means unwarranted in epic style' (Bartlett, *op. cit.*, p. 88). Should we consider as episodes such passages only as present no link whatever with the main narrative, we are bold to say that there would not be any of them in *Beowulf*. The passages in Klaeber's list are, of course, relatively, rather than purely, episodical, and the problem for us lies precisely in the determination of the various links which connect those 'relative' digressions with the rest of the poem.

[3] Klaeber, *Beowulf*, p. liv.

shall now briefly examine what are the main aspects of the problem in the present state of *Beowulf* studies.

When the 'Liedertheorie' was flourishing,[1] its adepts considered the episodes as particularly fit to corroborate their views. That the episodes could be detached from the text and were but loosely connected, if at all, with the main narrative was indeed regarded as perfectly obvious. As a consequence, there was no doubt that they had been introduced by one or several interpolators. Thus the digressions proved an excellent basis for the theories of multiple authorship. Yet, even after the 'Liedertheorie' had reached its apex, and when it was gradually abandoned, most of the episodes were still thought of in terms of later additions or interpolations. Thus Henry Bradley, who sums up the case very neatly, thought that, apart from the Beowulf-Breca contest, all other episodes 'were introduced by some later writer, who had heard recited, or perhaps had read, a multitude of the old heathen songs, the substance of which he piously sought to preserve from oblivion by weaving it in an abridged form, into the texture of the one great poem which he was transcribing.'[2]

The patchwork theories are now decidedly on the wane; in their few modern revivals (or survivals) however, the digressions are still a precious basis and a rich source of argument. To take a characteristic example: Professor Boer, one of the recent and most ingenious champions of the patchwork theory, actually singled out, among the supposed different authors of, or contributors to, *Beowulf*, a so-called 'episode poet' responsible for most of the digressions.[3]

In the glorious days of the dissecting school, when the hunt for interpolations was reaching its climax (partly because the epics of Homer and Virgil had already been the object of a similar chase), the wish, as Klaeber rightly observed, 'was no doubt father to the thought.'[4] This, however, can hardly be said of the more recent attempts. The digressions, or part of them at least, must now appear as having something in them which is inappropriate or irrelevant to the main narrative. In consequence they must, in fact, be regarded as 'redundancies' detrimental to the poetic beauty of the epic, and this impression

---

[1] It was first systematically applied to *Beowulf* by K. Müllenhoff. Cf. 'Die innere Geschichte des Beovulfs', *Zeitschrift für deutsches Altertum*, 1869, pp. 193–244.
[2] Henry Bradley, *Encyclopædia Britannica* (article on *Beowulf*), 11th ed., III, p. 760.
[3] See Klaeber, *Beowulf*, p. ciii.   [4] *Ibid.*, p. cii.

is confirmed in a way by the critical opinion of some of the greatest modern *Beowulf* scholars, whom nobody could possibly suspect of even the slightest bias in favour of the dissecting school. Thus, R. W. Chambers, at the beginning of the section devoted to a refutation of the dividers' arguments, allows that 'for the most part these digressions are not strictly apposite.'[1] Klaeber himself, whose penetrating remarks on the digressions throw a good deal of light on their relation to the general structure of the poem, admits that in the second part of the poem 'the disconnectedness caused by encumbering digressions is more conspicuous, episodic matter being thrown in here and there quite loosely, it seems, though according to a clearly conceived plan.'[2] Both Klaeber and Chambers, although strongly in favour of a unity of authorship in *Beowulf*, still admit in a way the possibility of some later additions, and they are not the only authorities holding the same opinion. If Chambers does not give us a precise instance of the kind, Klaeber, in his tentative reconstruction of the genesis of *Beowulf*, considers as likely that the digression on Hygelac, among others, is a later insertion, as it 'can easily be detached from the text.'[3]

To conclude on this point we shall say this. Modern dividers still consider most of the digressions as interpolations, whereas advocates of a unity of authorship, though they agree that a certain number of digressions (varying, of course, according to each individual case) are detrimental to the poetic value of *Beowulf*, are at variance as to the exact rôle which should be attributed to them in reference to the main story: estimates range from a certain degree of appositeness to a complete lack of relevance. Thus, as we have stated, the question remains quite open.

If, on the other hand, the digressions are considered from a historical standpoint, all divergences immediately vanish. The critics are unanimous in emphasizing the extreme interest of the digressions as documents concerning Germanic history and legend. Nay, Klaeber goes so far as to deplore 'that those

---

[1] R. W. Chambers, *Beowulf, An Introduction* . . . 2nd ed., Cambridge, 1932, p. 112. An echo of this opinion has found its way, quite recently, into the latest volume of the Oxford History of England: *Beowulf* 'is not, in fact, so much a story as a series of episodes in the life of a hero, interspersed with many digressions interesting because of their great age but often irrelevant' (F. M. Stenton, *Anglo-Saxon England*, Oxford, 1943, p. 194).
[2] Klaeber, *Beowulf*, p. cv.
[3] *Ibid.*, p. cvii.

subjects of intensely absorbing interest play only a minor part
in our epic, having to serve as a foil to a story which in itself is
of decidedly inferior weight.'[1] Such opinion is justified, but only
from the point of view of the historian.

After this brief retrospect, we shall now define our position
as clearly as possible. The object of the present essay is, generally
speaking, a systematic study of the digressions in *Beowulf*, from
a purely artistic point of view. We shall therefore not be
concerned, otherwise than incidentally, with their historical or
archaeological interest. The main questions which we shall
endeavour to answer are these: what part do the various digressions play in the poem considered as a work of art? In what
measure are they artistically justified, and what is their relation
to the structural (or spiritual) unity of the poem?

Now, whatever the answers, they are likely to involve
important consequences concerning not only an objective
appraisal of the nature of the digressions themselves, but also
such delicate questions as the unity of authorship, or even the
genesis of *Beowulf*. Those consequences, however, can only be
of any value at all if they result from a detailed and systematic
inquiry into all the digressions in the poem—such as has not
been done so far.

On the other hand, so as to avoid any bias or prejudice, the
question of authorship must remain open at the outset, and no
assumption will be made concerning that point at the beginning
of our study. Its only starting-point and basis is, strictly, the
text of the poem as it has come down to us. The single axiom
which is needed is that somebody was responsible for the text
as it stands. And as a corollary we shall say this: a given
digression may be the work of the original poet, of a mere
compiler, or of any kind of interpolator. But, in any case, the
man who introduced it certainly knew, or thought that he knew,
what he was doing; and it should be no impossible task to find
out his reasons, whatever may be the effect of the digression and
its ultimate value in the poem. It is therefore quite possible
that we may find a digression as representing a gross tampering
by an unskilful dabbler; but it is quite plausible, too, that
another digression may display the subtlety and mastery of a
real artist. The test of art is, as a matter of fact, the one test

---

[1] *Ibid.*, pp. liv-lv.

which we here claim as our main criterion.[1] We feel confident
that if it is applied systematically—though, of course, with as
little rigidity as possible—it might yield results substantial
enough to justify such a perilous enterprise.[2]

For clearness' sake we have provisionally divided the digressions into three main groups, according to the subject-matter.
The first, and more extensive, group is represented by such
digressions as concern moments in Beowulf's life and Geatish
history. All the historical (or legendary) digressions which are
not directly connected with Beowulf and the Geats have been
classed into a second group. The third group consists of those
digressions that are of a Biblical character. Those three principal
groups comprise all the digressions in *Beowulf* save the story of
Scyld and the Elegy of the Last Survivor which, owing to their
peculiar character, we find it more convenient to treat separately.

Such preliminary division—though somewhat artificial, of
course, suggests a first distinction between the general purpose
of each respective group of digressions, and is therefore useful
as an approach to the problem. Yet the actual part which must
be ascribed to the digressions in the poem transcends by far a
mere distinction of subject-matter, and a more discriminating
division should be attempted in accordance with the results of
our inquiry.

We shall now begin with the very first digression in *Beowulf*:
the origin of the Scylding line and Scyld's burial. As a kind of
episodic prologue it will provide a fit introduction to our
subject.

[1] And this may be attempted in spite of the too evident fact, pointed out by a critic,
that it is now 'practically impossible to be a very intelligent reader' of *Beowulf* (A. E. Du
Bois, 'The Unity of "Beowulf",' *Publications of the Modern Language Association of America*,
XLIX, 1934, p. 377).

[2] Miss Bartlett's conclusion on the narrative digressions in *Beowulf* deserves to be
noticed here. 'All the other passages [apart from the Finn lay] have some narrative,
even some dramatic significance. Not only are they not interpolations, they are not even
ecphrasis' (Bartlett, *op. cit.*, p. 88). Yet the examples of that narrative or dramatic
significance, as given by Miss Bartlett, are so briefly and roughly sketched that, though
pertinent, they are manifestly insufficient to give full support to such an important
conclusion. The whole problem is indeed well worth a detailed reconsideration.

THE DIGRESSIONS IN 'BEOWULF'

I. THE SCYLD EPISODE[1]

At a time when the Danes lacked a ruler, Scyld Scefing 'arrived as a little boy, alone and destitute, on the shores of the Danes; he became their king, a great and glorious chief, beloved by his loyal people; he conquered many tribes beyond the sea; he was blessed with a son; and when at the fated hour he had passed away, he was sent out into the sea with all the pomp of military splendor.'[2]   (ll. 1–52)

According to its subject-matter this episode would naturally be placed into our second group. Yet its situation at the very beginning of the poem, its peculiarity as an introduction to the epic, and the controversies to which it has given rise as such, rendered it more convenient to deal with it separately, at the outset of our study.

As is well known, the place of the story of Scyld as an original prologue to our epic has been challenged on various grounds. The main argument against its being a prologue seems to be derived from its supposed irrelevancy. According to Henry Bradley, the confusing effect of the extraneous episodes is indeed 'increased by a curiously irrelevant prologue. It begins by celebrating the ancient glories of the Danes, tells in allusive style the story of Scyld, the founder of the "Scylding" dynasty of Denmark, and praises the virtues of his son Beowulf. If this Danish Beowulf had been the hero of the poem, the opening would have been appropriate; but it seems strangely out of place as an introduction to the story of his namesake.'[3] Such an argument is certainly not without weight, at first sight, and to remove the discrepancy, Dr. Bradley was led to suppose that this prologue was 'the beginning of a different poem, the hero of which was not Beowulf the son of Ecgtheow, but his Danish namesake.'[4] To explain the transfer, moreover, Dr. Bradley surmises the existence of two rival versions: one—of which our prologue would be the surviving fragment—attributing the encounters with the monsters to Beowulf the Dane, the other to Beowulf son of Ecgtheow. This ingenious theory is supported (for lack of

---

[1] For the reader's convenience shorter digressions (i.e. less than twenty-five lines in length) are quoted *in extenso*. To save space, however, we only give a brief summary of longer digressions.   [2] Klaeber, *Beowulf*, p. 121.   [3] Bradley, *op. cit.*, p. 759.   [4] *Ibid.*, p. 761.

B

further evidence) by the fact that the first fifty-two lines of the prologue dealing with Scyld are left outside the numbered sections; as a consequence, 'it may reasonably be inferred that there once existed a written text of the poem that did not include these lines.'[1]

In his attempt at a reconstruction of the inner story of *Beowulf*, Professor Boer, one of the most 'daring dissectors' of the poem, presented different conclusions as to the origin of the prologue, yet agreed with Dr. Bradley that it could not have originally stood in its present place. For Professor Boer, the prologue was the opening of an old Dragon lay which was subsequently rehandled by a combiner. The combiner, after having substituted the Geats for the Danes in that Dragon lay, linked it to the Grendel part by composing 'Beowulf's Return', and transferred the prologue to the beginning of the whole concocted epic.[2]

It is difficult to undertake a criticism of Professor Boer's views concerning the prologue alone without entering at the same time upon a criticism of the whole theory of which the 'history' of the prologue is a part. Yet we may provisionally adopt the following attitude. Assuming, with some great *Beowulf* scholars, that it is hardly possible by means of internal evidence (or 'mere excision') only,[3] to disentangle and delimit with a sufficient amount of certainty the separate lays, poems, or interpolations, supposed to have been combined into the present *Beowulf* epic, we may admit that Professor Boer's theory, however ingenious it be and though not necessarily improbable in itself, must remain open to doubt. The same remark holds good of other similar attempts.[4]

If such conjectures as have so far been propounded to unravel the origin of the prologue can therefore be considered as un-convincing owing to a definite lack of positive evidence, the

---

[1] *Ibid.*, p. 759.

[2] See Klaeber, *Beowulf*, p. ciii. For a discussion of Prof. Boer's method and views, see R. W. Chambers, *Introduction*, pp. 424–30.

[3] *Ibid.*, p. 396.

[4] The most conspicuous of these is, of course, the important study of Berendsohn. Concerning the prologue, he assumes that in the first three lines 'der Anfang einer alten, ursprünglich dänischen Heldendichtung erhalten ist, der Eingang der Skiöldungen-Dichtung.' The introduction of Beowulf I., on the other hand, he ascribes to a so-called Grendel poet (W. A. Berendsohn, *Zur Vorgeschichte des 'Beowulf'*, Kopenhagen, 1935, pp. 248–49).

While paying a tribute to Berendsohn's investigations, and especially to his studies on the style of the poem, Klaeber is of opinion that 'considering the insufficient material at our disposal, the investigation as a whole—in a way, a refined and modified renewal of the old patchwork theories—could not lead to convincing results' (Klaeber, *Beowulf*, Supplement, 1940, p. 448).

actual problem of the prologue remains none the less unsolved. Even if the theories we have briefly examined were deemed untenable (and we shall for the present abstain from such an extreme judgment), the argument that the prologue is irrelevant does not, however, lose any of its weight. It would simply mean that an elucidation of the whys and wherefores of such irrelevancy has not yet been attained. Nothing prevents us from imagining that other theories might still be propounded with a similar purpose. And this will probably be the case as long as this irrelevancy is taken for granted. Indeed the core of the problem lies in that conception itself, and we propose to investigate it from an artistic point of view. If it could be shown that the irrelevancy is only apparent and that there are reasons for thinking that the present place of the prologue is artistically justified, then, and then only, would the problem be solved—and, as a matter of fact, by denying its existence!

By way of approach, it is only fair to pay tribute to the critic who has already gone a good way in that direction. In his sober objective treatment of the genesis of *Beowulf*, Professor Klaeber thinks that the original design of the author may have been limited to the Grendel part, or 'Bēowulfes sīð', and that the idea of a continuation setting forth the hero's death may have taken shape later. This, of course, is only a guess, but, be it as it may, Klaeber does not seem to object to the prologue as an opening to the Grendel part: 'the Danish court being the geographical and historical centre of the action, the poet not unnaturally started by detailing the Scylding pedigree and singing the praise of Scyld, the mythical ancestor of the royal line.'[1] Episodes dealing with events concerning the Scylding dynasty are indeed considered by him as 'a legitimate sort of setting.'[2] The fact that our prologue is left outside the numbered sections does not, to Klaeber, seem unnatural either: its being a kind of prelude would account for the fact.[3]

---

[1] Klaeber, *Beowulf*, p. cvi. In his paragraph on digressions and episodes, Professor Klaeber also writes: 'The glory of Scyld's life and departure forms a fitting prelude to the history of the Scyldings, who, next to the hero, claim our chief interest in the first part' (*ibid.*, p. liv). As to Miss Bartlett, she thinks that 'after all, one must begin a story somewhere, and, if the poet is going to begin with Hrothgar's dignity, an account of Hrothgar's line cannot be set down as episodic. Such a matter, perhaps, cannot be exactly determined' (Bartlett, *op. cit.*, p 86). Provided that one should be content with the explanation, the 'justification' it gives us of the Scyld prologue is, as in Professor Klaeber's case, restricted to the Grendel part. Denying that the story of Scyld is episodical is, by the way, a rather elegant solution of the problem.

[2] Klaeber, *Beowulf*, p. liii.   *Ibid.*, p. 121.

These hints of legitimization, however, concern the prologue as introductory to the Grendel part only, and not to the whole epic; a distinction which must be emphasized. As we have just said, Klaeber does not think it unlikely that the Dragon part might have been added later, and no superior unity of structure achieved: 'the lines in praise of the Danish kings placed as motto at the head of the first division and those extolling the virtues of the great and good Beowulf at the close of the poem typify, in a measure, the duality of subjects and compositions.'[1] Klaeber does not therefore defend the prologue as an opening to the whole poem: his conception of the genesis of *Beowulf* and of its duality shows on the contrary that, according to him, the prologue had no connection whatever with the Dragon part. So far at least its irrelevancy seems to be implied, and here Klaeber's position is, fundamentally, not very far from Dr. Bradley's.

On the other hand, the reasons given by Klaeber to legitimatize the prologue as introductory to the Grendel part are pertinent and valuable, drawn as they are from an artistic interpretation of that prologue: if any result is to be attained concerning the problem it must be sought along that line. Weighty as Klaeber's reasons are, I am not sure, however, whether further and more weighty reasons might not be adduced in favour of the prologue as prologue to the epic as a whole, and this *even if the Dragon part was originally included in the author's design.*

A connection between the prologue and the Grendel part seems to reside in a certain parallelism—which may not be devoid of a symbolic value—between Scyld himself and Beowulf, however different their respective missions. 'The Danes twice saved, or the double miracle of the House of Denmark'—this parody of a title would give the gist of what we mean here. The coming of Scyld, indeed, saves the Danes from one of the worst calamities which could possibly befall a people in the so-called Dark Ages: the lack of a ruler. The coming of Beowulf, on the other hand, saved them from the ravages of a fiendish monster who threatened the very existence of the Danes. Now both Scyld and Beowulf, though in different circumstances, come altogether unexpectedly, one might even say miraculously 'ofer swanrāde' to fulfil their mission; and if in the latter case the 'boundless sorrows' ('sīdra sorga')[2] to which

---

[1] *Beowulf*, p. cvii.   [2] *Ibid.*, l. 149.

Beowulf puts an end had already lasted for twelve years ('twelf
wintra tīd'),[1] in the former the 'dire distress' ('fyrenðearfe')[2] from
which the Danes are delivered by Scyld had likewise lasted for a
'lange hwīle' (i.e., probably several years too).[3] We are quite
aware that this suggested parallelism is more or less accidental
and that it is by no means so obvious as immediately to lead a
modern reader to think of Beowulf in terms of the second
liberator of the Danes, Scyld being the first. Yet other hints may
be detected that weave new tenuous threads—but even gossamers
are welcome when they lead us through the apparent maze of
Beowulf digressions—between Scyld and Beowulf. We have just
alluded to the miracle of both missions: in the case of Scyld
the miracle is glaring enough. Now if we turn to Beowulf's
victory over Grendel the miraculous element is stressed by
Hrothgar himself, in his great address in praise of the victorious
hero. The King's first thoughts express his gratitude towards
God, to whom he then pays the following significant tribute:
'ā mæg God wyrcan wunder æfter wundre, wuldres Hyrde.'[4]
Nothing prevents us, of course, from seeing in this *credo* a mere
tag with no purport whatever; yet I am not sure whether this
allusion to God's capacity of performing one miracle after another
might not imply at the same time an allusion to a former miracle
in Danish annals, namely the arrival of the 'God-sent' Scyld.
This seems the more likely in that it comes from the mouth of
Hrothgar who inherited the throne of Denmark as a great-
grandson of Scyld himself. There is a good chance, moreover,
that the hint would not be missed by the original audience of
the *Beowulf* poet, which was certainly more familiar with the
story of the Scyldings than we are. Such a hint may therefore
be regarded as providing a relevant link between the prologue
and the Grendel part.

Another hint of the same kind, perhaps even more elusive,
is to be found in another touch of parallelism between Scyld and
Beowulf. Although their youth was certainly different, it is
none the less characteristic that it stood in both cases in sharp
contrast to their glorious careers. Neither showed the slightest
promise of a brilliant future: Scyld was found a wretched and
abandoned child ('fēasceaft'), and Beowulf is conspicuous for
his inglorious youth.[5] Now the interesting point is that in both

---

[1] *Ibid.*, l. 147.   [2] *Ibid.*, l. 14.   [3] *Ibid.*, l. 16.   [4] *Ibid.*, ll. 930–931.
[5] The question of Beowulf's 'inglorious youth' is discussed at some length further
down, pp. 24–7.

cases the striking reversal in their fortunes is clearly stressed by
the poet. After a reference to Scyld's deeds 'syð ðan ǣrest
wearð fēasceaft funden,' the poet adds:

> hē þæs frōfre gebād,
> weox under wolcnum weorðmyndum þāh,
> oð þæt him ǣghwylc ymbsittendra
> ofer hronrāde hȳran scolde,
> gomban gyldan[1]

Closing Beowulf's report to Hygelac by a few lines in praise of
his hero, the poet, on the other hand, mentions that in his youth
Beowulf was despised by the Geats, 'swȳ ðe (wēn)don, þæt hē
slēac wǣre, æðeling unfrom.' Yet, as in the case of Scyld,
'Edwenden cwōm tīrēadigum menn torna gehwylces.'[2] Natural
as it is in such circumstances, this emphasis on a parallel contrast
is none the less noteworthy.

It is even more remarkable owing to the character itself of
that contrast. Whenever the poet alludes to a reversal in the
epic in general, it is decidedly in an opposite sense from good
to bad (in accordance with the general mood of the poem).
This is particularly conspicuous, as we have already shown
elsewhere, in the case of a series of anticipations, all hinting at a
future disaster in contrast to present glory and magnificence.[3]
But it is not only in actual anticipations that the 'edwenden'
hinted at takes such a course. Let us only mention the allusions
to Heremod, who gave promise of such a brilliant career: 'ðēah
þe hine mihtig God mægenes wynnum, eafeþum stēpte, ofer
ealle men forð gefremede', and none the less ended quite
miserably, 'drēamlēas gebād, þæt hē þæs gewinnes weorc
þrōwade, lēodbealo longsum.'[4] Indeed, had Heremod been
known to him, or had he not been so rudely interrupted,
Chaucer's monk might very well have included him in his 'roll
of dismal biographies.' It should be added that the Knight
himself could hardly have found in Beowulf contrary examples

---

[1] Beowulf, ll. 7–11.　　　　[2] Ibid., ll. 2187–2189.
[3] 'The Use of Anticipations in "Beowulf",' Review of English Studies, XVI, July,
1940, p. 299.
[4] Beowulf, ll. 1716–1718, 1720–1722. In that speech—as Professor Bonnard pointed
out to me—Hrothgar addresses Beowulf in words which are strangely reminiscent of
those the poet had used when speaking of Scyld:

> ðū scealt tō frōfre weorþan
> eal langtwīdig lēodum þīnum,
> hæleðum tō helpe.
>
> 　　　　　　　　(1707–1709)

more striking (and so much more comforting) than the parallel
cases of Scyld and Beowulf.

Although we shall deal again with the Heremod episode, we
may point out here that the very mention of Heremod's reign
gives us another link between the prologue and the Grendel
part. What we may gather with certainty from the way in which
Heremod's reign is alluded to is that its story must have been
very well known at the time when *Beowulf* was composed. Had
this not been the case the reader would certainly have missed
the meaning of that passage, a meaning which still appears to us
half-hidden in spite of the researches of modern historians.
Now it may be safely admitted that Heremod's death was
followed precisely by the interregnum which put the Danes
under such terrible stress.[1] Consequently the mere mention of
Heremod's death would thus almost inevitably lead the audience's
thoughts to that 'ealdorlēase' period of Danish history and the
miracle of Scyld's arrival.

Such links as we have examined so far are, if we may say
so, mere cross-references. However valuable and not to be
discarded, the connection does not entail the slightest interaction
or modification between the objects thus connected. Another
link, on the other hand, may be found which brings with it a new
and important element.

As Klaeber stressed in his notes concerning the story of Scyld,
'his illustrious career fittingly foreshadows the greatness of his
royal line.'[2] Now this glorification of the Scylding line can easily
be explained by various and very obvious reasons. Not only
because the Scyldings 'next to the hero, claim our chief interest
in the first part',[3] where their glorification thus contributes to
the splendour of the setting, but also because that glorious
prelude heightens the effect of Grendel's attacks, threatening to
bring to a disastrous end the last years of Hrothgar's reign, the
venerable heir to such a magnificent dynasty. Indeed, just as
the glory of the Danes under Scyld and his son stood out in
sharp contrast to their miserable state when they lacked a king,
the glorious reign of Hrothgar, worthy of the great tradition,
emphasizes by contrast the sorrowful plight in which he and his
people find themselves in consequence of Grendel's attacks.

[1] In Anglo-Saxon and Norse Genealogies, for instance, 'Heremōd figures as the
father, i.e. predecessor of Scyld' (Klaeber, *Beowulf*, p. 164).
[2] *Ibid.*, p. 121.
[3] *Ibid.*, p. liv.

This leads us to another artistic purpose in the glorification of the Scyldings. Had the distressing condition of the Danes, their total incapacity of escaping the woes inflicted upon them by Grendel and of getting rid of the monster, served as the only introduction to Beowulf's mission and fight, this would have created an impression of mere weakness on the part of the Danes. Such an atmosphere of unqualified weakness and misery would inevitably have threatened to spoil, or at least to diminish at the outset, the very greatness of Beowulf's enterprise. But if we remember—thanks to the extremely vivid and striking prologue —that we have before us not only a king successful in wars and builder of a hall, but the actual heir of so glorious a line reigning over a glorious people, then Beowulf's undertaking is given its true epic greatness. It is precisely because the Danes do not play so glorious a part in the poem that their inherent greatness had to be so vividly set forth in a brilliant introduction: the impression, then, of Grendel's attacks is of an almost insuperable calamity, the victims of which still keep their dignity and valour intact—and this enhances the glory of Beowulf himself.[1] That this conception has much to be said for it is corroborated in a way by an interpretation of the Ecgtheow episode.

So far we have examined only such links as render the prologue artistically apposite to the Grendel part. The question of its relevance to the Dragon part (and therefore to the poem as a whole) is, of course, much more delicate. The duality in the structure of *Beowulf*, to which most critics refer as an established fact, seems to exclude even the possibility of a connection between the prologue and the second part of the poem. Indeed, the setting of the Grendel part,—the court of the Danes—which rendered an allusion to the foundation of the Scylding line so natural at the outset, is now definitely abandoned, and the action shifts to the home of the Geats; and whatever glimpses we catch of Geatish history in the Dragon part are in no way connected with the Danes. No wonder that

[1] Speaking of the method of description by contrast, Miss Blomfield writes: 'As a structural principle, it may be traced in the antiphonal exordium. We hear first of the mighty destiny and wide fame of the Scyldings. The crescendo of Scylding power rouses opposing forces of cunning evil ever lurking to reverse the prosperity of mankind; by Grendel's raids the fame of the Scyldings is blasted, the utmost human effort frustrated, the mightiest of rulers made impotent. Beowulf is then introduced in the all-powerful enterprise of untried youth' (J. Blomfield, 'The Style and Structure of "Beowulf",' *Review of English Studies*, XIV, 1938. pp. 397–398).

the story of Scyld has seemed to many out of place in connection with that second part of the epic. But here, much more than in the Grendel part, the connection with the prologue—if connection there is—is not 'historical', i.e., does not involve relations which can be delimited in time and space, or characterized by the cause-effect relationship, but is rather 'transcendental', i.e., it depends purely on the subtle laws of artistic effect.

The story of Scyld, sent by God to the lordless Danes, has a 'historical' character inasmuch as it throws some light on the origin of the royal house reigning over the Danes at the time in which the action takes place; and as the Danes are in the foreground in the whole of the Grendel part, the connection is so obvious that it might justify a brief narration of that story. It acquires, however, a 'transcendental' character if viewed on another plane, as a highly significant parallel and contrast to that fine piece of epic prophecy concerning the future downfall of the Geats themselves, left 'lordless' after Beowulf's death. Indeed, at the very beginning and at the very end of the poem looms the spectre of a 'lordless' time, that worst calamity in Germanic times. The fact that the former was miraculously put an end to by the foundation of a glorious dynasty, whereas the latter is fraught with the blackest forebodings of an implicit catastrophe, is in perfect harmony with the general mood of the poem. We may say that if the rise of the Scyldings is the prologue to the epic, its counterpart, the fall of the Geats (announced by Beowulf's death) is in a way its epilogue.

This is admirably brought out, and in a particularly effective manner, by the corresponding funeral scenes. Viewed in that light and in their striking contrast, they are endowed with a real symbolic value which heightens the artistic effect and the unity of the whole poem.

Far from being steeped in a dark atmosphere of woe and sadness, the whole beautiful description of Scyld's funeral leaves, on the contrary, an impression of brilliancy and splendour which sets the traditional reference to the mourning of the retainers far in the background. Indeed, the magnificent picture of the ship, the body of the king in its bosom, 'on bearm scipes', by the mast, a ship laden with treasure and setting out on the waves to a mysterious destination with the royal banner floating on its mast, is almost an apotheosis. It suggests a beginning and is the symbol of a glorious future.[1] What a striking contrast with Beowulf's earthly funeral: not only is its whole atmosphere more depressing and sorrowful, but Beowulf's mound itself suggests a terminus. It symbolizes the end of a glorious past, while the future is fraught with black and uncanny forebodings. Thus interpreted, that contrast is, perhaps, one of the finest artistic achievements in the poem.

Before dealing with further episodes, we may now briefly draw a few provisional conclusions. Such interpretation as we have ventured to give of the Scyld episode does not necessarily favour one of the numerous assumptions concerning its composition and its place in the inner history of the poem as against another. Indeed, it may be said to be compatible with most of them. If we should suppose, for instance, that it was written by the interpolator responsible for Beowulf's Return,[2] it is simply to that man that such a high degree of artistic skill is to be attributed—and considering his ingenuity in linking the Grendel and the Dragon part, this would by no means appear impossible. Yet the great advantage of our interpretation is that it renders the Scyld prologue quite compatible also with the assumption that it was originally written by the *Beowulf* poet and destined from the beginning to occupy the place in which it now stands. This, of course, would be both the simplest and most satisfying conception, as it leaves intact the text as it has come down to us, and implies no complicated process of interpolation. An artistic

---

[1] The relation between the symbolic aspect of Scyld's burial in *Beowulf* and the actual practice of ship-burial is well worth examining. As Professor Hoops sums up, 'der Schiffgräber-Periode, die etwa 500 n. Chr. beginnt, ging wahrscheinlich eine Periode vorauf, in der die Leiche im Schiffe beigesetzt und dem Meer übergeben wurde' (J. Hoops, *Kommentar zum Beowulf*, Heidelberg, 1932, p. 12). Such was then the usual practice in the first phase of ship-burial, and the *Beowulf* poet, whose 'antiquarian interest' has been pointed out, knew how to revive it in his picture of Scyld's funeral. Yet it has been remarked that the poet did not speak of setting fire to the ship as was also the practice. 'Some conceive the ship-burial as being carried out without firing, and that is clearly the poet's belief. It is evident from the nature of things that it cannot be shown that it was not so, but our other descriptions include firing, and I doubt if a different method would be employed when the practice was alive.' Professor Girvan then points out the inconveniences which a mere driving out to sea of the funeral ship would have entailed (Ritchie Girvan, *Beowulf and the Seventh Century*, London, 1935, pp. 33–34). As a matter of fact we suggest that it was the poet's purpose of using it as a symbol rather than his possible 'belief' which dictated the motive of the driving out to sea without firing. If both practices were actually used, he probably chose the one which best suited his purpose. But even if we assume, with Professor Girvan, that the method including firing was alone employed, might not that aspect have been consciously omitted and the account—to use Professor Girvan's own sentence in reference to another question—thus 'distorted in the interests of poetry'?

[2] Professor Schücking's opinion at the time when he developed his 'special thesis' on *Beowulfs Rückkehr*.

justification of the episode, such as we have attempted by removing its supposed irrelevancy to the rest of the poem, suppresses at the same time the greatest obstacle to that conception.

Be that as it may, and whatever position is assumed towards the problem, we hope, at any rate, that this interpretation is capable of shedding some light on new aspects of the art of *Beowulf*.

II. DIGRESSIONS CONCERNING EPISODES OF BEOWULF'S LIFE AND GEATISH HISTORY

THE presence of a group of digressions concerning sections of Beowulf's biography is, perhaps, the easiest to account for. Most, if not all, of them may be considered in fact to 'contain welcome information about the hero's life.'[1] Their exact relation to the rest of the poem as well as their artistic value is none the less well worth some further inquiry.

The delicate point is the relation between a digression and the main action. Strictly speaking, and owing to its very nature, no digression is indispensable to the evolution of the main action; and, considered from that point of view, any digression could therefore be suppressed without entailing the slightest loss to the normal evolution of that action. Yet, if not necessary, digressions may be very useful and may contribute to the value of the work of art: they may add to the colouring of a poem, they may provide—just as some digressive scenes in a play—a welcome relaxation from a tension; they may also serve as a foil to a given situation and, in some cases, possess a symbolic value contributing to the actual effect and understanding of the poem itself; all this apart from their intrinsic interest which may be very great. So great, indeed, that it may be the only reason for the presence of many a digression: and this is the danger in the use of the device. For its interest, however great it may be, can never wholly justify, by itself alone, the use of a digression: it is quite appropriate in a conversation, and lends much to its charm, but not in a work of art where a digression should always be subordinate to a greater purpose, linking it to the rest of the poem. Then only can a digression be considered as actually justified: far from endangering the unity of the poem, it then contributes to its artistic effect. The use of digressions is often a question of delicate balance. Yet this makes of them a very subtle instrument in the hands of a real artist.

To revert to *Beowulf*, we have already said that the intrinsic interest of many of the digressions (especially their historical interest) is so great that all critics are thankful for their existence while in many cases uttering strong misgivings as to their

---

[1] Klaeber, *Beowulf*, p. liii.

appositeness. The problem is therefore essentially—we must repeat it—to know in what degree the digressions can be considered as artistically justified.

1. Beowulf's Fight against the Giants (419-424)

Beowulf tells Hrothgar that the wise men advised him to go to Denmark because they knew his strength:

> selfe ofersāwon, ðā ic of searwum cwōm,
> fāh from fēondum, þǣr ic fīfe geband,
> ȳðde eotena cyn, ond on ȳðum slōg
> niceras nihtes, nearoþearfe drēah,
> wræc Wedera nīð—wēan āhsodon—,
> forgrand gramum.
>
> (419-424)

The first digression of the group is the very short mention of a glorious feat in Beowulf's early life: the fight against the giants and the 'niceras.' Its immediate purpose is evidently to inspire confidence in the success of Beowulf's enterprise by giving a first illustration of his uncommon strength, and to give at the same time a sort of justification for Beowulf's arrival at the Danish court. It thus gives a first confirmation of the earliest reference to Beowulf in the poem, who was presented as 'Hygelaces þegn' in the following words: 'sē wæs moncynnes mægenes strengest on þǣm dæge þysses līfes, æþele ond ēacen.'[1] It also suggests in a nutshell the double aspect of Beowulf as a specialist in fighting monsters as well on earth as on sea, to which further reference will be made in the poem, and which makes him particularly apt for a fight with Grendel and his mother.'[2]

In fact, that digression is immediately followed by a reference to Grendel: 'ond nū wið Grendel sceal, wið þām āglǣcan āna gehēgan ðing wið þyrse.'[3]—so that the link is unmistakable. That digression, therefore, should not be separated from the Breca episode, of which it is but a forerunner.

---

[1] *Beowulf*, ll. 196-198.
[2] As Professor Schücking puts it: 'Ähnlich rühmt sich Beowulf, dessen Dreissig-Männerkraft ihr.. schon einen titanischen Zug gibt, nicht des Sieges über irdische Gegner, sondern dessen über Seeungeheuer, die seinem Volk zu schaffen machten (423) und die er in schweren nächtlichen Wasserkämpfen vollkommen ausrottete. Durch solche einzigartige Leistungen hat er sich gewissermassen die Berechtigung zu dem geplanten Grendelkampf erworben' (L. L. Schücking, 'Heldenstolz und Würde im Angelsächsischen,' *Abhandlungen der Philologisch-Historischen Klasse der Sächsischen Akademie der Wissenschaften*, Leipzig, 1933, XLII, No. V, p. 37).
[3] *Beowulf*, ll. 424-426.

Yet this is only one aspect of the digression, the more obvious. Another and more subtle purpose may, perhaps, be assigned to it, making it at the same time a forerunner also of the Ecgtheow episode in its real significance. As such it should also be treated together with that episode.

If one compares the account of Beowulf's departure to Denmark in his own speech before Hrothgar with that of the narrator himself, a slight, but interesting, point arises. In the poet's account Beowulf's decision to sail to Denmark comes from the hero himself: 'cwæð, hē gūðcyning ofer swanrāde sēcean wolde, mærne þēoden, þā him wæs manna þearf';[1] the 'snotere ceorlas' are simply said—if the litotes is rightly interpreted—to encourage him warmly in his resolution and to watch the omens (which are, of course, understood to be favourable). Beowulf's own account does not show any discrepancy with it, yet there is a slight and perhaps significant change of emphasis: the decision is no longer presented as originally coming from Beowulf himself, but rather from the 'wise men'. Even if we should suppose it as understood (from lines 409–10) that Beowulf made up his mind to go and fight Grendel before the matter was discussed with them, the 'wise men' are decidedly given a greater share in the whole scheme than in the poet's account: 'þā mē þæt gelærdon lēode mīne,' quoth Beowulf, 'þā sēlestan, snotere ceorlas, þēoden Hrōðgār, þæt ic þē sōhte, forþan hīe mægenes cræft mīn[n]e cūþon.'[2] The verb 'gelæran' makes it here particularly clear. Now we think that this change of emphasis is not entirely due to mere chance. Though a 'boasting word' is perfectly in its place and almost conventional in the mouth of an epic hero, and often occurs in the course of the poem, a certain amount (or even an appearance) of modesty was no less advisable at this particular point of Beowulf's first address to Hrothgar. Had Beowulf, who was simply 'Hygelaces thegn', appeared before Hrothgar and announced to him point-blank that he had resolved to leave his country and come to the Danish court to cleanse the royal hall of the monster, that moreover he had already tried his hand at a few giants and sea-monsters, this would have involved a certain abruptness which might have appeared slightly unpleasant on the part of a young man towards a venerable king who had proved himself—and his men as well—unable to get rid of the monster. The very

---

[1] *Beowulf*, ll. 199–201.   [2] *Ibid.*, ll. 415–418.

slight shade of presumption, or let us say the appearance of unconscious superiority which might have been involved in such a presentation, almost entirely vanishes in the form it has now taken in Beowulf's speech. As the rumours of Grendel's depredations had spread to the Geats, it was the 'wise men' among them who had advised (or persuaded) Beowulf to go and fight him; *they* were aware of Beowulf's strength and had seen how he had overcome giants and niceras. The result is the same, yet the form, or let us say the style, makes the difference.

Such an interpretation might, perhaps, appear too far-fetched if the Ecgtheow episode which immediately follows Beowulf's speech (and the present digression by some thirty-five lines only) were not there to give us a glaring illustration of the element which we think was already contained here in germ.

2. THE ECGTHEOW DIGRESSION (459–472)

At the end of his speech Beowulf told the king of his strong determination to fight the monster. In his reply to Beowulf's address, the king does not immediately begin with the story of Grendel's depredations, but first devotes fourteen lines to a particular incident in the life of Beowulf's father:

> 'Geslōh þīn fæder fæhðe mæste;
> wearþ hē Heaþolāfe tō handbonan
> mid Wilfingum; ðā hine Wedera cyn
> for herebrōgan habban ne mihte.
> þanon hē gesōhte Sūð-Dena folc
> ofer ȳða gewealc, Ār-Scyldinga;
> ðā ic furðum wēold folce Deniga
> ond on geogoðe hēold ginne rīce,
> hordburh hæleþa; ða wæs Heregār dēad,
> mīn yldra mæg unlifigende,
> bearn Healfdenes; sē wæs betera ðonne ic!
> Siððan þā fæhðe fēo þingode;
> sende ic Wylfingum ofer wæteres hrycg
> ealde mādmas; hē mē āþas swōr.'
>
> (459–472)

Had not Beowulf's arrival to fight a monster that they themselves were entirely unable to get rid of, and the acceptance of foreign help for this purpose, contained the possibility of wounding the pride of the Danes, we have good reason to believe that there would have been neither an Ecgtheow nor even perhaps an Unferth episode.

It is not without some definite purpose, indeed, that in his welcome and answer to Beowulf's address—Hrothgar devotes more than a third of his speech to the recollection of the Ecgtheow incident. Even if a mention of Beowulf's father should, for its own sake, have been thought appropriate in Hrothgar's mouth, and to create one more bond between Beowulf (or the Geats) and the Danes, it might have taken a dozen different forms rather than that one. It might have been, for instance, a laudatory reference, implying the greatest expectations from the offspring of so glorious a stock as Ecgtheow's. Or, to indulge in a second guess, the poet might have put in Hrothgar's mouth an allusion to such heroic feats on the part of Ecgtheow as might have appeared suitable to foreshadow Beowulf's own exploits. Moreover, had the poet kept in mind Beowulf's greatness only, a further reference to the tidings of Beowulf's early achievements, having already preceded him at the Danish court, would have been the best introduction to Hrothgar's speech.[1]

Yet, and this is the interesting point, the whole reference is to a situation which is not particularly laudatory for Beowulf's father, and the real emphasis is laid on Hrothgar's own help and good offices having saved him when under particularly great stress. We therefore cannot but approve of Professor Hoops's excellent psychological interpretation which illuminates the ultimate significance of the whole episode. 'Hrothgar beginnt seine Ansprache damit, dass er auf den Gegensatz hinweist zwischen der Art, wie Beowulf an den dänischen Hof kommt, und der, wie einst sein Vater kam: "Du kommst, uns zu helfen,— dein Vater kam einst als Hilfsbedürftiger: *Geslōh þin fæder fæhðe mæste* etc." Dadurch wird das Peinliche für die Dänen, dass der König fremde Hilfe annimmt, gemildert: Beowulfs Hilfe ist gewissermassen der Dank für das, was Hrothgar einst für seinen Vater getan hatte.'[2]

---

[1] Such a reference is to be found in Hrothgar's answer to Wulfgar's message announcing the arrival of the Geats (ll. 377–381).

[2] J. Hoops, *Beowulfstudien*, Heidelberg, 1932, p. 98. This can also be found, expressed in almost identical terms, in the *Kommentar zum Beowulf*, p. 72.

Another purpose of the passage is to add a significant trait to Hrothgar's character: 'Vielmehr zeigt sich Hroðgar hier als der rechte "rex pacificus," dessen Stolz im Friedenstiften beruht . . . So hat er die 'ordinata concordia' zwischen den Staaten, die nach Augustinus das Ziel der guten Obrigkeit sein soll, herbeigeführt und erntet jetzt deren Früchte' (Schücking, *Heldenstolz*, pp. 34–35).

We are even tempted to go farther than Professor Hoops and suggest—as we hinted before—that one aspect at least of the Unferth episode should be interpreted in the light of such a psychological situation.

3. THE UNFERTH INTERMEZZO (499–603)

In the course of the festivities, Unferth, who was jealous of Beowulf's fame, 'onband beadurūne' by asking the hero if he was the Beowulf who engaged in a swimming contest with Breca. After both young men had struggled for seven nights against the wintry waves of the sea, Breca finally won the race (he was stronger than his comrade). Therefore Unferth expects little success from Beowulf if he dares fight against Grendel.

In his reply Beowulf gives a detailed report of his adventure with Breca: sword in hand—to fight against sea-monsters— the young men swam together for five nights; Breca was not faster than Beowulf, and Beowulf himself did not want to abandon his companion—it was the flood and the north wind that separated them in the darkness of the night. Beowulf had to fight against sea-monsters and killed nine of them until he was borne by the floods on the shores of the Finns. For aught he knows such deeds have never been told of Unferth or of Breca— it was only known that Unferth had killed his own brother. As to Grendel, he would never have committed so many horrors in Heorot were Unferth so fierce a fighter as he boasted. Yet the monster will soon get acquainted with the strength of a Geat.   (499–603)

If the Ecgtheow digression in a way counterbalances the fact that the Danes are accepting foreign help from Beowulf, this might not necessarily remove at one and the same time any trace of misgiving or jealousy among the Danes concerning Beowulf's capacities and ability to cope with so difficult a task. It may be said in fact that Unferth gives voice to such misgivings as Beowulf's arrival would naturally call forth among some at least of the Danes—and this is in no way incompatible with Hrothgar's dignified and courtly address to Beowulf. 'If Unferth's manners seem to indicate a lapse from the high standard prevailing at the court of Hrothgar, they must be looked upon as an inheritance from a ruder age,' writes Professor Lawrence.[1] Yet it is not even

[1] W. W. Lawrence, *Beowulf and Epic Tradition*, Cambridge, Mass., 1930, p. 153.

C

necessary to assume such a return to a ruder age in spite of the
probability that the episode comes right down from former
legends or lays. As Professor Lawrence himself stresses a few
lines further, 'the poet has carefully motivated Unferth's resent-
ment. . . . It irritates him [Unferth] that a distinguished foreigner
has come to slay the demon which no Dane has been able to
dispose of.'[1] Now the expression of so natural a sentiment in
such circumstances could evidently not be uttered on Beowulf's
arrival, and following Hrothgar's welcoming address. There
it would have been really out of place. But once the festivities
are well under way and beer has been generously poured out,
no wonder that one of the thanes 'onband beadurūne' and gave
vent to his inner feelings.

The fact that this part has been attributed to Unferth by the
poet is not devoid of significance. It has sometimes been looked
upon as surprising that such words eminently contrasting with
the refined courtesy characteristic of Hrothgar's court should
have been put in the mouth of so prominent a person as Unferth,
who occupied a seat of honour at the king's feet. Yet it is
precisely because of his prominent position (as well as of his own
character) that, of all the Danes, Unferth was the man peculiarly
liable to resent Beowulf's expedition. As long as no one proved
able to meet Grendel in fight, Unferth—who apparently did not
venture to measure himself against the monster—could still
enjoy the position of undisputed superiority which he was eager
to maintain. The existence of Grendel could not deprive him
of his glory: the monster simply transcended human powers.
Beowulf's attempt was robbing him of his foremost place, and
Unferth's first reaction was naturally enough spite and jealousy.
We hear from Beowulf's speech that Unferth prided himself
on his valour: 'gif þīn hige wǣre, sefa swā searogrim, swā þū
self talast.'[2] Yet in spite of Beowulf's biting allusion to Grendel's
security, we should not take this as an entirely idle vaunt of some
miles gloriosus. The poet's reference to Unferth, just after the
Finnsburg episode, makes it clear. Unferth is again presented as
occupying his usual place of honour: 'æt fōtum sæt frēan
Scyldinga'; yet there is a new element: he is not called 'thyle'
only, but his great courage and valour in battle are specifically
stated: 'hē hæfde mōd micel . . ..'[3]

[1] *Ibid.*, *loc. cit.*   [2] *Beowulf*, ll. 593–594.
[3] *Ibid.*, ll. 1166a, 1167–1168. Cf. note 5, p. 19.

In fact the poet showed a fine sense of appreciation in representing Unferth as a distinguished and glorious thane in spite of his earlier attack: it indirectly (and effectively) adds to Beowulf's greatness. Had Unferth been reduced to a mere swashbuckler, Beowulf's superiority over him would not have meant so much as it actually does, nor would have the lending of the sword. The very attitude of Unferth, further on in the poem, which has been a matter of numerous comments and interpretations, becomes very clear and simple (and artistically quite skilful) if we keep in mind that its principal purpose is to serve as a foil and emphasize Beowulf's greatness. Unferth, foremost of Danish warriors, whom we have seen so jealous of his own glory, being actually led to acknowledge with great sincerity, and publicly, Beowulf's superiority—what a tribute to Beowulf! Apart from the allusion to Unferth's courage and loyalty referred to above, the very fact that *he* was in possession of 'Hrunting', the sword so marvellous that 'næfre hit æt hilde ne swāc . . . folcstede fāra'[1] is a flaming confirmation of his own valour. Yet he has found a better than himself, and notwithstanding a first movement of despite, overcomes his jealousy, and finally admits the fact quite openly.

The transition, moreover, is skilfully managed. First (l. 980) a brief allusion after Beowulf's victory over Grendel: Unferth remains silent, which is tantamount, as Klaeber finely remarks, to 'er schämte sich'.[2] Then, when Beowulf undertakes the even greater task of fighting against Grendel's mother, Unferth is completely won by the hero's greatness. As a sign of his admiration, and to make up for his former attack, he lends him the precious sword. 'Mighty in strength', the son of Ecglaf, 'hūru ne gemunde . . . þæt hē ǣr gespræc wine druncen' (again rightly interpreted by Klaeber as a litotes for he 'repudiated his taunting speech').[3] And yet there only comes the significant passage: 'selfa ne dorste under ȳða gewin . . . þær hē dōme forlēas, ellenmǣrðum.'[4] What he did not dare to undertake, Beowulf did: Unferth, therefore, 'lost his glory', i.e., could no longer appear as the first and foremost fighter, second to none.[5]

[1] *Ibid.*, ll. 1460–1463.
[2] F. Klaeber, 'Unferð's Verhalten im Beowulf,' *Beiblatt zur Anglia*, LIII, 1942, p. 271.
[3] *Beowulf*, ll. 1465–1467. Klaeber, *loc. cit.*
[4] *Beowulf*, ll. 1468–1471.
[5] The fact that Unferth did not 'lose his glory', or at least kept his prominent position, though he is said to have killed his brother, makes it likely that he did not act as a coward in that particular (and quite obscure) drama.

This also throws retrospective light on his former attitude. That *mea culpa* is the more effective, coming from a man of great valour, and enhances all the more Beowulf's extraordinary capacities. At the same time, and by this very attitude, Unferth gains our sympathy and we cannot but applaud the final friendly scene.[1] We may add, therefore, that the attempts to represent Unferth in a way as the villain of the piece[2] are wide of the mark in *Beowulf*—artistically they lack any firm basis.

To revert to Unferth's first reaction, we may repeat that, psychologically, and considering the real situation, the whole process is entirely justified. The poet well perceived what opportunity the situation gave him—and, we are bold to say, made the best use of it. Indeed, the effect produced by the Breca contest—the main purpose of which is, by means of a vivid narrative, to complete our information as to the hero's exceptional character—is much more effective, both from a psychological and a dramatic standpoint, if introduced by the Unferth incident.

Psychologically, because the narration put in the hero's mouth of one of his earlier exploits is thus given a definite motivation. It is all the more skilfully introduced and appears all the more effective in contrast to Unferth's slandering version. It also gives a vivid illustration of a new quality—and not one of the least—in Beowulf. The mighty hero, slayer of sea-monsters and giants, is given an opportunity to show that he is a match for any courtier, 'þēah [his] wit duge!'[3] His answer to Unferth is indeed a little masterpiece of the kind. First a good-humoured yet pretty sharp allusion to Unferth's too generous

---

[1] As Klaeber concludes, 'der Umstand, dass Unferð seine Unterlegenheit einsieht und trotzdem, neidlos, dem Bēowulf zu einem neuen Siege behilflich sein will, setzt den hochherzigen Charakter seiner Handlungsweise jedenfalls in helles Licht' (*op. cit.*, p. 272).

[2] In his *Danmarks Heltedigtning*, indeed, Olrik not only considers Unferth as the personification of the evil counsellor but thinks that he may well have been responsible for the later conflict between Hrothulf and Hrothgar's sons. (See Hoops, *Kommentar*, pp. 76–77.)

Professor Girvan likewise supports Olrik's views and thinks that Unferth was invented for the Hrothwulf story: 'He is the embodied attitude of Hrothwulf . . . the personification of a sentiment, in this case Hrothwulf's jealous hatred' (R. Girvan, *op. cit.*, p. 67).

[3] This has been emphasized by Professor Schücking: 'Der Held soll seinem Gegner— das ist wohl der Sinn— auch im Zugenkampf durchaus gewachsen sein. Indem er aber seiner Herr wird, ohne es zu Tätlichkeiten kommen zu lassen, erweist sich auch seine Selbstbeherrschung' (Schücking, *Heldenstolz*, p. 38).

At the same time Professor Schücking thinks that the poet wanted to give his audience, whose eagerness for spectacular adventures had been excited by a previous short allusion, a further and more detailed illustration of Beowulf's fabulous feats. More difficult, however, is the question whether the poet wanted his hero to appear as a good story-teller: such a tendency would not be easy to prove (*ibid.*, *loc. cit.*). The dialectic force of Beowulf's answer is, at any rate, striking enough.

drinking, then his own version of the Breca contest. This version is characterized by Beowulf's calm, objective, yet lively, account of the whole incident as it actually happened, rectifying without passion but with great persuasive force Unferth's tendentious and distorted version.[1] The difference in tone between the first thrust at Unferth and the narration itself is conspicuous. Now when the story has come to a close, culminating in the great fight against the sea-monsters (the actual climax of the daring enterprise), Beowulf skilfully introduces the second thrust against Unferth by opposing, with biting irony, this his fight to Unferth's sinister exploit as a fratricide. Yet the final thrust has been reserved with a fine sense of gradation: the allusion to Grendel's impunity, told with a certain leisure full of grim humour, by putting the emphasis on the very cause of Unferth's discontent, certainly cuts to the quick and gives Unferth the *coup de grâce* in the 'wit-combat'. The strong determination to fight Grendel as quickly as possible and give him his due is, finally, the counterpart of Unferth's misgivings and prophecy of failure at the close of his speech.

The Unferth incident also heightens the dramatic value of the Breca episode: it should not be forgotten that we know very little of Beowulf when he comes to the Danish court. But for the brief allusion to his early fights with the 'niceras' and the giants, we have not been told anything about exceptional deeds of his. He has simply been presented to us as the strongest man alive. Now, although we know Unferth's sentiments when he launches his attack, his narration of the Breca incident is not devoid of a certain effect on the reader: his claim that Beowulf and Breca engaged in a race, and the very details he gives about how the latter outstripped the former, are wholly plausible;[2] and that is, of course, in contradiction with what *we* expect of Beowulf. If this is not enough, however, to shake our confidence in Beowulf's strength and valour, it leaves us none the less all the more eager to have the apparent contradiction solved, and hear

[1] This new aspect of Beowulf's character, as displayed in his repartee to Unferth's attack, has been finely brought into relief by Professor Schücking who sees in it perhaps the main motivation of the episode: 'Prüfstein des Mannes ist ferner vor allem sein *Verhältnis zu den irasziblen Trieben*. Er muss 'continens in ira' sein. Ihn so zu erweisen ist vielleicht der Hauptgrund der Einschaltung der Unferth-Episode im Epos gewesen. Wohl wehrt er energisch die Anpöbeleien des Frechen ab, aber er lässt sich doch keineswegs zu Tätlichkeiten gegen ihn hinreissen, sondern zeigt sich seiner selbst sicher und macht sich ihn bald gar zum Freunde' (L. L. Schücking, 'Das Königsideal im Beowulf', *Bulletin of the Modern Humanities Research Association*, III, No. 8, October, 1929, p. 153).

[2] Lawrence, *Beowulf and Epic Tradition*, p. 156.

the hero's rectification. Beowulf's own version, then, has the greater effect of fully satisfying our expectations, and in such a way that it considerably increases our opinion and esteem of the hero.

As for the Breca story itself—independently of its presentation and introduction—its ultimate value is, of course, to exalt our hero and strengthen our confidence in Beowulf's ability to cope with the fearful monster.'[1] By its emphasis on Beowulf's extraordinary capacities as a swimmer and a fighter of terrible sea-monsters (Beowulf has risen, in our opinion, to the status of an expert in such matters), it is a vivid illustration and amplification of the hint given in lines 419–424, already pointed out.

We may therefore consider that not only the whole digression is entirely appropriate, but that, artistically, the three digressions are linked together with a fine dramatic movement. At the outset we have a first slight intimation of Beowulf's future success: the brief allusion to his early exploits and the attitude of the wise men give us a clear hint of the hero's unusual strength. Then the address of King Hrothgar, somewhat diffident at first and hinting at the debt the hero's father had contracted, yet honouring his guest by the official and hearty acceptance of his help—a fact which implicitly fortifies our hopes in the final success. Suddenly, the unexpected contrast of Unferth's attack which entails some misgivings as to the supposed unmatched strength of Beowulf and consequently a clear prophecy of failure. Owing to the circumstances and character of Unferth, it does not shake our confidence, yet strikes a discordant note, and by apparently contradicting our first impression excites our attention and asks for a solution confirming that first impression. This confirmation immediately follows, and by contrast the effect of Beowulf's counter-attack gains in force. It reduces to naught the traces of misgivings and at the same time effectively illustrates and emphasizes Beowulf's capacities, already implied in the first episode.

The dramatic prologue is at an end: from now on the action itself may begin.

4. THE FALL OF HYGELAC (1197–1214)

The scop has just recited the tale of Finn; convivial mirth rises again; then Wealhtheow, after having addressed the King

---

[1] Klaeber, *Beowulf*, p. 148. See also B. Haeuschkel, *Die Technik der Erzählung im Beowulf-liede*, Breslau, 1904, p. 64.

and Hrothulf, presents Beowulf with costly jewels. The poet
compares them to the wonderful necklace of the Brisings:

> Nænigne ic under swegle sēlran hȳrde
> hordmāðum hæleþa, syþðan Hāma ætwæg
> tō þære byrhtan byrig Brōsinga mene,
> sigle ond sincfæt,—searonīðas flēah
> Eormenrīces, gecēas ēcne rǣd.—
> þone hring hæfde Higelāc Gēata,
> nefa Swertinges nȳhstan sīðe,
> siðþan hē under segne sinc ealgode,
> wælrēaf werede; hyne wyrd fornam,
> syþðan hē for wlenco wēan āhsode,
> fæhðe tō Frȳsum. Hē þā frætwe wæg,
> eorclanstānas ofer ȳða ful,
> rīce þēoden; hē under rande gecranc.
> Gehwearf þā in Francna fæþm feorh cyninges,
> brēostgewǣdu, ond se bēah somod;
> wyrsan wīgfrecan wæl rēafedon
> æfter gūðsceare, Gēata lēode
> hrēawīc hēoldon.

(1197–1214)

As there are several allusions to the Frankish expedition in
the poem, we shall provisionally examine the present digression
as an independent unit, leaving to a later inquiry the task of
connecting the different digressions on Hygelac (and more
generally on the Swedish wars) and showing what part they
play in the poem as a group.

From a restricted viewpoint we may say that this first allusion
to Hygelac's disastrous raid gives us a fine instance of a particular use of contrast characteristic of *Beowulf*. We already
called attention to it elsewhere, when studying the artistic
value of anticipations in our epic. 'It is always when something looks or is described as splendid, stable, or peaceful, or
when friendly people are in the midst of rejoicings' that anticipations of sad events or catastrophes take place.[1] Allusions to the
burning of Heorot, and the Heathobards episode are particularly
striking illustrations of this. But this is not strictly restricted
to anticipations, and although less typical than these cases,
it is none the less characteristic that this first hint of Hygelac's

---

[1] See *Review of English Studies*, XVI, July, 1940, p. 299.

fall should have been called up by the description of the wonderful treasures bequeathed to Beowulf after this twofold and glorious victory. So wonderful, in fact, that 'nænigne ic under swegle sēlran hȳrde hordmāðum hæleþa.'[1] It almost looks as if there were already here some latent implications of the same nature as those to be met with in the Dragon story, where the very beauty and prodigious riches of the Dragon hoard stands out in contrast to the curse attached to it. Here, the 'neck-ring' is among the finest on earth . . . yet Hygelac had it when he was slain: 'Hē þā frætwe wæg, . . . hē under rande gecranc.'[2] The touch is slight—as the poet wanted it to be—yet it is already the germ of the tremendous implications which will grow out of the repeated allusions to Hygelac's downfall in the course of the epic.

Leaving Hygelac for a moment on his 'nȳhstan sīðe' we shall now briefly deal with the episode referring to Beowulf's early youth.

5. Beowulf's Inglorious Youth (2183–2189)

After Beowulf's report to Hygelac, the poet has a few lines in praise of his hero and then abruptly refers to his sluggish youth:

> Hēan wæs lange,
> swā hyne Gēata bearn gōdne ne tealdon,
> nē hyne on medobence micles wyrðne
> drihten Wedera gedōn wolde;
> swȳðe (wēn)don, þæt hē slēac wǣre,
> æðeling unfrom. Edwenden cwōm
> tīrēadigum menn torna gehwylces.
>
> (2183–2189)

That the 'sluggish youth' motive is a remnant of folk-tales can hardly be denied, and the parallels with Grettir and Ormr Storolfsson which have been repeatedly pointed out are significant enough. This fact, however, is not sufficient by itself to account for the presence of such an element here. If the poet kept that legendary trait, we may assume that he had some reasons for doing so.

Obviously enough this element is but another touch contributing to the glorification of Beowulf that the poet did not

---

[1] *Beowulf*, ll. 1197–1198.   [2] *Ibid.*, ll. 1207, 1209.

want to miss. A first hint of this is that it follows close upon the Beowulf-Heremod parallel—a conspicuous tribute to Beowulf's qualities—and is destined to complete the picture by way of a further contrast.

If a poet wants to make something of his hero's youth, he may do it in two different ways. The more immediate and obvious one is to present the hero already as a first-class prodigy in his early youth: one of the oldest and most typical illustrations of the case is that of young Hercules strangling the snakes in his cradle! The other way, which already smacks faintly of a device, is, on the contrary, to present him as either sluggish or apparently blunt, and insist on his being despised by his comrades only to heighten the effect of the glorious deeds by which he reveals himself, and make them the more conspicuous and remarkable by way of an unexpected (and highly relished) contrast: just as the hero was thought inferior to his contemporaries, he now transcends them all by far—a dramatic element which cannot but serve the cause of the hero as it in no way diminishes our high opinion of him.[1] We may even consider as a modern survival of the device the not unfrequent tendency of the biographer to emphasize with obvious delight the fact that his famous man was at the very bottom of his form at school and exult in representing some authoritative people, and especially his master, calling him a dunce in his youth . . . The anecdote is so far from being detrimental to its hero in the eyes of the general reader that the great man himself is often the first to indulge in it. Of course, we have also at times the other type, i.e., the young prodigy; but this is precisely the point: there is generally no middle way (at least when 'legend' interferes); either the hero was an early prodigy or he was a dunce.

To leave modern 'hagiography' and come back to Beowulf, we see that, curiously enough—and though it seems something of a paradox—both traits have been used, in some measure at least, in the epic. But this has been done so skilfully as not to produce the effect of a paradox.

Early in the poem, when Beowulf introduces himself to Hroth-

---

[1] That this is the effect intended by the poet is also Miss Blomfield's opinion: 'The theme [i.e. the advancement of Beowulf's career] is brought out still further by innuendoes defining knightly conduct by contrast (2,166-169, 2,177-183), and is finally closed on the dominant of Beowulf by a description of his boorish beginnings (2,183-188)—a fact we learn only when it is introduced to heighten Beowulf's eminence and substantiate the comment that a *tireadig mann* will always make good' (J. Blomfield, 'The Style and Structure of "Beowulf",' *Review of English Studies*, XIV, 1938, p. 402).

gar, he alludes to youthful exploits: 'hæbbe ic mǣrða fela on-gunnen on geogoþe.'[1] He therein shows himself true to the epic tradition, and together with the reference to the early fights with monsters this serves as a kind of 'curriculum vitae' justifying his claim to come and challenge Grendel. Now not only is the allusion to Beowulf's inglorious youth separated from this justification by some seventeen hundred lines (which is more than in the case of some discrepancies in the age of a dramatic hero), but it does not necessarily conflict with it: the 'mǣrða fela ongunnen on geogoþe' may very well represent, for instance, a first series of heroic deeds by which Beowulf revealed himself, giving the lie to general opinion—yet while he was still young in deed. There are degrees after all in youth, and the 'edwenden' itself seems to be referring to probable successes anterior to those we hear from his own mouth. It should also be pointed out that in another of his speeches Beowulf himself refers to early fights: 'Fela ic on giogoðe gūðræsa genæs, orleghwīla.'[2] But even if this be not admitted—and we quite agree that it is a matter of conjecture—there is another reason why we cannot, on this point, follow Professor Klaeber when he writes that 'the introduction of the commonplace story of the sluggish youth is not very convincing',[3] or that the motive has been 'somewhat awkwardly' added,[4] and this probably owing to its apparent contradiction to lines 408–9, to which Klaeber also refers.[5] Both allusions, if viewed within their respective contexts, are in fact in perfect keeping with it.

In the first part of Beowulf's address recapitulating some high deeds on the eve of a new glorious undertaking, the reference to the youthful exploits is but the first hint that announces the theme (and the allusion, moreover, is not specific enough to exclude the possibility of a less brilliant period having preceded this, a hint of which would, of course, have been quite out of place). The allusion to the 'inglorious youth', on the other hand, can only be fully appreciated if considered as a direct sequence to the Heremod parallel: both, in fact, form a rather close unit, the object being the glorification of the hero. In the parallel, the evil deeds of Heremod serve as a foil to Beowulf's

---

[1] *Beowulf*, ll. 408–409.
[2] *Ibid.*, ll. 2426–2427.
[3] Klaeber, *Beowulf*, p. 207.
[4] *Ibid.*, p. xxvii.
[5] Miss Bartlett likewise refers to 'the account of Beowulf's sluggishness—which does indeed appear misplaced' (Bartlett, *op. cit.*, p. 88).

own qualities,[1] and although implicit the contrast is evident enough. But this is only the one half of the diptych: the allusion to Beowulf's 'inglorious youth' which follows is itself in direct contrast to the Heremod case. Beowulf was first thought sluggish and was despised for a time, but 'edwenden' came, and what 'edwenden': he has now grown into one of the most famous and glorious heroes of his time, and is about to add new fame to his brilliant career. Now any reader of, or listener to, the poem acquainted with the story of Heremod (and we have every reason to think that those for whom *Beowulf* was written were familiar with it),[2] would immediately grasp the contrast which the poet left implicit: in Klaeber's own words, 'Heremōd was a strong, valiant hero, pre-eminent among his fellows, giving promise of a brilliant career, but subsequently proved a bad ruler . . . and having become a burden to his people, ended miserably.'[3] Thus we have indeed a poor beginning followed by a prodigious ascent contrasted with a brilliant promise ending in a miserable downfall! This again has a fine dramatic effect, and required no mean artistic sense.[4]

[1] Cf. ll. 2177–2183. 'Deutliche Anspielung auf Heremod, der nach 1713 f., *brēat bolgen- mōd bēodgenēatas | eaxlgesteallan*' (Hoops, *Kommentar*, p. 238).

[2] The story of Heremod has been described, in fact, as 'a mere succession of allusions intended for an audience who knew the tale quite well' (Chambers, *Introduction*, p. 90).

[3] Klaeber, *Beowulf*, p. 162.

[4] This effective contrast is perhaps the strongest argument in favour of our interpreta- tion: and this leads us to keep to that interpretation in spite of Professor Malone's interest- ing and plausible explanation to which it is opposed. A short discussion of Professor Malone's theory will not be out of place here.

Not only does Professor Malone endorse Klaeber's opinion that the introduction of the story is unconvincing, but he thinks that we may go further and that the poet actually 'made nothing of the motif, that he tried, indeed, to explain it away' (Kemp Malone, 'Young Beowulf', *Journal of English and Germanic Philology*, XXXVI, Jan., 1937, pp. 21–22). At the basis of Professor Malone's argument is his particular conception of the chronology of young Beowulf's development. In a first stage, 'he seemed to the Geats a youth of the greatest promise. Secondly, the hero becomes aware of his obligations to God, and refuses to use his strength for anything trivial; . . . during this stage he falls out of favor at home;' knowing his strength, his companions 'attribute his inactivity to sloth and want of spirit. Thirdly, the hero hears of Grendel and realizes that his call has come. He announces his purpose, and his fellow-Geats . . .are delighted to see the mighty man come out of his lethargy' (*ibid.*, p. 23).

Against such a chronology several objections may be advanced. Nothing allows us to declare with certainty that the motive of the boorish beginnings represents a *second* stage. Connecting that motive, as has been done by Malone, with Beowulf's self-control and restraint does not seem quite convincing: those qualities (corresponding, as Professor Schücking showed, to the ideal of *mensura* or *sobrietas*) are always presented as, or at least, felt to be, among the very greatest which can ever be attained. To bring that home was perhaps the main purpose of the Beowulf-Heremod parallel, and—this is the important point—no passage in the text shows that these qualities are not considered as such by Beowulf's fellow-Geats. The litotes on Beowulf's forbearance (2179–2183) are a last and implicit touch of the contrast with Heremod (who represents the *tyrannus* possessed of *superbia*), and the fact that it is followed by the allusion to the sluggish youth does not

6. Hygelac's Death in Friesland, Beowulf's Return by Swimming and his Guardianship of Heardred; the Second Swedish Wars (2354–2396)

Beowulf has made up his mind to fight alone against the Dragon. We are told that he did not fear the beast as he had gone through many a perilous fight since he overcame Grendel and his dam.

Then the poet tells us how Beowulf escaped from Friesland, where Hygelac had been slain in battle, by swimming back to his country with thirty suits of armour in his hands, and how he declined the Queen's offer of the throne, preferring to act as a counsellor to young Heardred until the prince was old enough to assume the leadership of the Geatish kingdom.

Later on Heardred fell in a war against the Swedes, together with one of the Swedish princes (sons of Ohthere) who had taken refuge at the Geatish court. Thereupon Beowulf ascended the Geatish throne and helped Eadgils to avenge his brother; in that new phase of the Swedish-Geatish war, the king of the Swedes (Onela) was killed.

(2354–2396)

necessarily mean that it was owing to that admirable restraint of his, supposedly mis-apprehended by the Geats, that Beowulf was despised for a time. The opposition is rather between the *present* glory of Beowulf and his popularity (once more made tangible by the Heremod parallel) and the period *long since gone* of temporary 'low esteem' which may be put as well in his very early youth (rather as a first stage, and preceding the first youthful exploits). That the poet did not mention the motive before (say in reference to Beowulf's *enfances*') would simply show that he kept it in store for a time when it would be more effective: and effective it is when introduced, as it is here, 'to heighten Beowulf's eminence' (Blomfield, *loc. cit.*) by contrast! The allusion to the wise men who little blamed that expedi-tion 'þēah hē him lēof wǣre' (202–203) may simply be considered as litotes meaning that they approved very highly of the enterprise (because they knew well enough of what Beowulf was capable and what feats he had already accomplished, see lines 415 ff.) rather than a delight at seeing him come out of his supposed lethargy. If lethargy there was, it probably took place before the glorious feats referred to in ll. 415 ff. which had already endeared Beowulf to the 'snotere ceorlas'. This, of course, cannot be proved any more than Professor Malone's assumption that it was a second phase. Yet our conception has another and a last advantage still.

To account for the fact that the *Beowulf* poet had to try and explain away the motive—whereas it would have been so simple to omit it, provided that it had proved a nuisance—Professor Malone is led to declare that having found the motive in his source-material the poet, 'conscientious monk that he was, found himself unwilling to cast it aside' (*ibid.*, p. 22). We think that the *Beowulf* poet, however conscientious, was too much of an artist to keep such a detail got from his source-material unless he could use it to good pur-pose. As we have attempted to show, it was actually used to good purpose indeed—and that is why the poet did not reject it.

Both explanations, by the way, are not quite as opposed as they seem: we have tried to show how the poet used the motive artistically, Professor Malone showed how he explained it away . . . artistically!

The immediate object of this digression is again the glorification of Beowulf by a reference to one of his sensational earlier deeds.

The reference is cleverly introduced. It can be paralleled, in a way, to the first allusion to a Beowulfian exploit made in the poem: there is something similar at least in the situation. Before undertaking to fight Grendel Beowulf alludes, in his address to Hrothgar, to early successes against monsters justifying, in a way, his audacious enterprise. Now just when Beowulf has resolved to deliver his own people from the terror of the Dragon and kill the monster, the poet, this time, makes a kind of recapitulation of some of the greatest of his hero's previous feats: Beowulf did not falter indeed, as he had already found himself under great stresses ('forðon hē ǣr fela nearo nēðende nīða gedīgde')[1]—briefly referring to the fight with the 'Grendel family', then to the Frisian expedition.

It should be pointed out, however, that this little review of Beowulf's exploits is here given a particular dramatic value which makes of it almost a piece of dramatic irony. These former successes, in fact, are set forth just after the poet has told us in anticipation that the hero would find his death as well as his enemy in this his last and greatest fight:

> Sceolde lǣndaga
> æþeling ǣrgōd ende gebīdan,
> worulde lifes, ond se wyrm somod[2]

This foretelling of Beowulf's death on the eve of his great undertaking throws a grim shadow on this recollection of his great prowess—just as the knowledge of his downfall renders Napoleon's greatest victories even more dramatic to an admirer.

That the Grendel adventure is merely mentioned incidentally is due to the fact that the poet obviously did not want to re-tell it a third time! But is it possible to know why, among a series of other adventures and fights, the poet now chose the Frisian expedition? Is there some ground which may be said to justify that particular choice—or is it merely taken as a sample of Beowulf's heroic deeds and nothing more?

Let us first remark that as a sample of Beowulf's capacities it illustrates once more his remarkable skill as a swimmer, and is in perfect accord with his marvellous display in the

---

[1] *Beowulf*, ll. 2349–2350.   [2] *Ibid.*, ll. 2341–2343.

Breca incident. But the choice of this episode transcends by
far that simple element and is to be judged by the considerable
importance of the immediately succeeding events and their
real consequences, the complete significance of which can only
be fully grasped towards the end of the poem. Yet so much is
clear already at that point: the fall of Hygelac leaves the Geatish
throne vacant and brings about Hygd's offer of the crown and
kingdom to Beowulf on his return from Friesland. The offer is
even more important than it seems: it makes it already clear
that the Queen herself, who in this circumstance puts the welfare
of her people above considerations of family, sees in Beowulf
the only man (now that Hygelac is dead) capable of defending
them against foreign enemies. She therefore prefers him to her
own son: 'bearne ne truwode, þæt hē wið ælfylcum ēþelstōlas
healdan cūðe, ðā wæs Hygelāc dēad.'[1] This allusion to 'ælfylcum', so full of implications and forebodings, must be remembered, as the threat is going to loom larger and larger, and there
will come a time when Beowulf's death will confirm Hygd's
worst fears and premonitions. But more of this later on.

This offer of the crown—and this is its immediate effect—
gives the poet an excellent opportunity to illustrate Beowulf's
moral greatness after having emphasized his fabulous strength
and skill in 'sundnytte'. Beowulf's refusal of the crown in favour
of a kind of regency—assisting the young prince with friendly
counsels—is not only a remarkable example of disinterestedness
and loyalty in itself, but it is cleverly made even greater by its
implicit contrast with the particular situation at the Danish
court which can be deduced from the poet's subtle allusions.[2]
A perfect concord is said to reign among the Danes, and yet
several anticipatory hints foretell sinister happenings. 'At a
later time . . . as the poet intimates . . . the harmonious union
was broken, and Hrōþulf, unmindful of the obligations of
gratitude, behaved ill towards his cousins, Hrēðrīc and Hrōð-
mund, that is to say—very likely—usurped the throne. One is
tempted to regard Beowulf's 'adoption' as in some way connected

---

[1] *Beowulf*, ll. 2370–2372.
[2] See especially the following lines:

þā cwōm Wealhþēo forð
gān under gyldnum bēage þǣr þā gōdan twēgen
sǣton suhtergefæderan; þā gȳt wæs hiera sib ætgædere,
æghwylc ōðrum trȳwe.   (1162–1165)

as well as ll. 1018–1019, 1178 ff. and 1228 ff.

with the anticipated treachery of Hrōþulf.'[1] Kemp Malone interprets Wealhtheow's emphasis[2] on the concord and loyalty among the Danes as a piece of dramatic irony and thinks that the poet expected his audience to know the story ending in Hrothulf's murder of Hrethric and usurpation of the Danish throne. An interpretation which Hoops finds likely enough.[3]

Thus this story of the Danish succession serves as a foil to Beowulf's attitude towards the Geatish succession: on the one side we have a treacherous attempt to get hold of the throne by killing (or at least supplanting) the legal successor, on the other a refusal to accept the crown (offered by the Queen Mother herself) out of sheer loyalty towards the rightful heir.

The second part of the episode is devoted to an event in the Swedish wars. Beowulf's refusal having led to Heardred's accession, the poet could not but mention the early death of the young king which finally put Beowulf himself on the Geatish throne. The link with the preceding part of the episode is thus natural enough. Now the circumstances of Heardred's death allow the poet to introduce for the first time the Swedish wars in the poem, wars of which we are to hear with an alarming recurrence! This in its turn permits us to detect further links with the first part of the episode. Hygd's fear of 'aelfylcum' are here dramatically confirmed, as the Swedish raids find their outcome precisely in her son's death. At the same time her trust in Beowulf is also justified by Onela's retreat, who does not seem particularly eager to fight against Beowulf, now that the hero has ascended the Geatish throne ('lēt ðone bregostōl Bīowulf healdan'!)[4] Thus by showing so conspicuously how Hygd's confidence in him was well placed, the second part of the episode also serves the cause of Beowulf. The purpose of the poet is to convey the certitude that Beowulf's power was enough not only to repel any invader but even to prevent any attempt at an invasion, even on the part of a hereditary foe—the Swedes, of course.

We must already observe here that the poet wants us to concentrate on the Swedes as an immediate background to the central happenings (the fight with the Dragon). And this by means of a series of episodes: from now on—and this is the

---

[1] Klaeber, *Beowulf*, p. xxxii.   [2] 1180 ff.
[3] See Hoops, J., *Kommentar*, p. 153. Professor Schücking also refers to the passage as 'ein Stück tragischer Ironie' (*Heldenstolz*, p. 42).
[4] *Beowulf*, l. 2389.

illuminating point—*there will be no other episode in the poem not connected with the Swedish wars*! What this really means will be seen later.

It should also be remarked, finally, that the story of Onela and his brother's sons Eanmund and Eadgils provides another (and this time much closer) foil to Beowulf's attitude towards Heardred: the rightful heirs to Ohthere are indeed deprived of the throne by their uncle Onela—a further instance of usurpation sharply contrasting with Beowulf's loyalty and 'delicacy'.

7. KING HRETHEL, THE END OF HEREBEALD, THE EARLIER WAR WITH THE SWEDES, BEOWULF'S SLAYING OF DAEGHREFN IN FRIESLAND (2426–2509)

Beowulf tells his faithful retainers that he was seven years of age when he came to the court of his grandfather, King Hrethel, who loved him as much as his own sons Herebeald, Hæthcyn and Hygelac. The eldest son, Herebeald, was accidentally killed by his own brother Hæthcyn, and this misfortune breaks the heart of the old King. Hrethel's sorrow is compared to that of an old man whose son has been hanged.

Upon the King's death, the Swedes, led by Ongentheow's sons, attack the Geats and cause severe damage in the country. Then Hæthcyn and Hygelac undertake an expedition of revenge against the Swedes, in the course of which both Hæthcyn and the 'old, terrible' Swedish king are killed.

Beowulf concludes this retrospect by expressing his determination to fight for his people as he has always done and as long as the sword holds out, which he took from Dæghrefn, the Frankish warrior killed by him in Friesland.

(2426–2509)

This episode, which contains two distinct parts, is all contained in Beowulf's farewell address. This speech, which is the hero's last before the great fight, is naturally enough a kind of retrospect of his life in the form of a survey, but with a certain perspective which is well worth noticing. Here again the choice of the events and the emphasis that is laid on them have their meaning. What comes out in a particularly conspicuous way is the impression of the impending doom, an impression which is as yet simply suggested, not imposed. This is made quite clear if we compare this episode with the preceding one with which it has some outward similarities.

The present episode is also introduced with an allusion to early fights (compare ll. 2426–27 with 2349–51) leading to the narration of some memorable event. But whereas it was the author who narrated those events, the recollection of which was given a singularly dramatic value as he had just told us of the imminent death of his hero in the coming fight, this time the foreknowledge (or at least presentiment) of his death is extended to the hero himself:

> Him wæs geōmor sefa,
> wæfre ond wælfūs, wyrd ungemete nēah,
> sē ðone gomelan grētan sceolde,
> sēcean sāwle hord, sundur gedælan
> līf wið līce; nō þon lange wæs
> feorh æþelinges flæsce bewunden.[1]

The appearance of 'wyrd' here is of great importance as it gives us the keynote not only of the episode but of the whole ending of the poem.

This foreknowledge, on the part of the hero, is bound to play no mean rôle in the development of the great speech: the gradation between the two episodes is, in fact, remarkable. In the former, the events illustrating Beowulf's capacities and qualities are definitely in the foreground and are still narrated in the 'old style' if we may say so, i.e. rather in the heroic manner; though our newly acquired knowledge of the hero's fate throws its dramatic shadow on them, they are still endowed with a great brilliance and a sort of epic mood. In the latter there is quite another perspective: Beowulf's personal actions stand in the background and are rather briefly mentioned towards the end, only to serve as a 'prop' to a kind of profession of loyalty and courage, whereas a sort of 'episode within the episode', in which Beowulf only played the part of a spectator, is allowed to occupy the foreground. And this story was chosen with a particular sense for situation. Not only is the tone perfectly in accord with Beowulf's 'geōmor sefa' but the theme itself is a striking and sombre illustration of the action of 'wyrd'. It is no longer in the heroic or epic mood, but in an elegiac and deeply melancholic tone. The very prominence implicitly given to 'wyrd'

---

[1] *Beowulf*, ll. 2419–2424.

D

on the one hand—the accidental killing of Herebeald by his
brother's hand suggests the inexorability of fate—and, on the
other hand, the poignant atmosphere of grief and sadness in
which the 'Father's Lament' is steeped, prepare the central
theme and dominant mood of the end of the poem and thus
artistically justify the first part of the episode.

Yet, if Beowulf's own sad mood and intimation of his
approaching end is doubly felt (in the poet's words and in the
theme of the hero's speech and elegy), it must not give the
impression of weakening in the slightest way the hero's resolve:
'heroic-elegiac poem' was the critic's definition of *Beowulf*—
heroic-elegiac, also, is this important episode.

The heroic strain comes again in the second part with its
narration of another aspect of the Swedish wars in which
Beowulf resumes the part of an actor—and this allows him to
stress his firm resolution to fight now, just as he had done
in those circumstances, in the forefront (2497 ff.). Just as
Beowulf fought with courage and loyalty on the side of his
liege, now he is going to fight as a king for his own people. This
continuity of the hero's fighting career and this unswerving
fidelity to his own ideal provide indeed a fine conclusion to
Beowulf's speech.[1] As a critic remarked, Beowulf was true to

---

[1] There is no serious reason, therefore, to see in that conclusion a contradiction with
the passage of the hero's dying speech in which he makes a brief survey of his merits in
life, before 'the imminent meeting with his Maker.' This in spite of Mr. Pons's question:
'N'y a-t-il pas aussi incompatibilité entre cette sorte d'examen de conscience profondément
chrétien qui précède la mort de Beowulf (2730-51) et l'insouciance totale de l'au-delà, le
seul désir fanfaron de tenter la chance et de conquérir l'or que manifeste le héros immé-
diatement avant le combat . . .' (E. Pons, *Le Thème et le Sentiment de la Nature dans la Poésie
Anglo-Saxonne*, Strasbourg, 1925, p. 56). As must be remembered, the elements of Beowulf's
greatness reside both in his legendary strength and courage and in the moral qualities
required of a *rex justus*. It is only natural that just before the Dragon fight the traditional
Beowulfian courage and resolution should once more be emphasized in much the same way
as before the preceding fights. If we remember, on the other hand, that Beowulf had an
intimation of his approaching end in the fateful combat, yet did not falter in his resolve,
can his attitude ('ne bið swylc earges sið!') be described as 'désir fanfaron de tenter sa
chance'? Though the moral qualities are given a prominent place in the retrospect of the
dying man—as was natural under the circumstances—the other aspect is not entirely omitted
either: when he emphasizes that no enemy ever dared attack him during his long reign,

> Ic ðas leode heold
> fiftig wintra; næs se folccyning,
> ymbesittendra ænig ðara,
> þe mec guðwinum gretan dorste,
> egesan ðeon.   (2732b-2736a)

we know that it was owing, above all, to that renowned strength and courage of his which
he once more revealed in that supreme fight.

This attitude of Beowulf before the Dragon fight, in which the characteristic element of
personal dignity is so remarkable, is not only the same as before the Grendel fight, but it is
also adopted by Byrhtnoth just before the outset of the battle of Maldon. Professor Schück-

the Horatian precept 'Servetur ad imum Qualis ab incepto processerit.'[1] This conclusion is once more expressed in brief in the very last words of the speech, words which the author has taken care to detach from the rest of the discourse as a sort of *leitmotiv* and echo:

> Ic geneðde fela
> gūða on geogoðe; gȳt ic wylle,
> frōd folces weard fæhðe sēcan,
> mærðu fremman . . .[2]

At the same time as this retrospect allowed that fine profession of the hero's fidelity towards his own self and his own ideal, it gave the poet an opportunity to harp once more on the Swedish wars. That the recurrence of the allusions to the Swedish wars is part of a conscious and lucidly designed plan is also suggested by the next episode, dealing as it does with Weohstan's slaying of Eanmund.

8. Weohstan's Slaying of Eanmund in the Later Swedish-Geatish War (2602-2625)[3]

Beowulf's companions have abandoned him to save their lives. Only one of them stands firm when he sees his king in distress:

> Wīglāf wæs hāten, Wēoxstānes sunu,
> lēoflīc lindwiga, lēod Scylfinga,
> mæg Ælfheres; geseah his mondryhten
> under heregrīman hāt þrōwian.
> Gemunde ðā ðā āre, þē hē him ǣr forgeaf,
> wīcstede welige Wǣgmundinga,
> folcrihta gehwylc, swā his fæder āhte;
> ne mihte ðā forhabban, hond rond gefēng,

---

ing, who called attention to the parallel, therefore regards this attitude as 'ein typisches Motiv der Epik' and finds a similar element precisely in Beowulf's dying words: 'Derselbe Geist aber, in dem hier das hingenommen wird, dem man nicht entrinnen kann, lebt auch in den . . . Abschiedsworten des sterbenden Beowulf, die persönliche Würde bleibt eben auch Gott gegenüber gewahrt' (L. L. Schücking, *Heldenstolz*, p. 22).

[1] W. Thomas, *Beowulf et les premiers Fragments épiques Anglo-Saxons*, Paris, 1919, p. xxx.

[2] *Beowulf*, ll. 2511-2514.

[3] This section has already been published in a slightly different form. See *English Studies*, XXVII, February, 1946, pp. 14-19.

geolwe linde, gomel swyrd getēah;
þæt wæs mid eldum Ēanmundes lāf,
suna Ōhthere[s]; þām æt sæcce wearð,
wræcca(n) winelēasum Wēohstān bana
mēces ecgum, ond his māgum ætbær
brūnfāgne helm, hringde byrnan,
ealdsweord etonisc; þæt him Onela forgeaf,
his gædelinges gūðgewædu,
fyrdsearo fūslīc, — nō ymbe ðā fæhðe spræc,
þēah ðe hē his brōðor bearn ābredwade.
Hē [ðā] frætwe gehēold fela missēra,
bill ond byrnan, oð ðæt his byre mihte
eorlscipe efnan swā his ærfæder;
geaf him ðā mid Gēatum gūðgewæda,
æghwæs unrīm, þā hē of ealdre gewāt
frōd on forðweg.

(2602–2625)

Apart from the voluntary stressing of the Swedish theme, the reasons for the choice of this episode are more difficult to establish. There is in it, however, a latent parallelism with a point of the preceding episode that weaves a tenuous but tangible link of relevance betraying once more the hand of the artist.

We must first briefly recall the main purpose of the introduction of the character of Wiglaf in that part of the poem. According to Klaeber, 'the introduction of an associate in the person of Wīglāf served to provide not only a welcome helper in the fatal struggle, but an eyewitness and assistant at the king's pathetic death, besides an heir and executor who directs the impressive closing scene of the poem.'[1] This is quite pertinent, and such reasons are an ample justification of the part of Wiglaf. Yet there is something more in Wiglaf: the fact that he is Beowulf's kinsman not only puts him in the position of heir and testamentary executor—which is of greater importance than appears at first sight—but indirectly serves the cause of Beowulf himself. In fact one cannot help feeling that had this part been played by any other Geat, Beowulf's heroic courage would not, of course, have lost its exceptional quality; it would have been, let us say, matched by an 'ordinary' human being.

[1] Klaeber, *Beowulf*, p. xxii.

Now Wiglaf is evidently no 'ordinary' human being, he is of the same blood as Beowulf—and mark the emphasis of the poet: 'sibb' æfre ne mæg wiht onwendan þām ðe wēl þenceð.'[1] In other words, *bon sang ne peut mentir*! Therefore Wiglaf's own courage is in some sort a reflection of Beowulf's exceptional valour which thus still remains on an inimitable height. This should, perhaps, be brought into connection with the contrast between it and the conduct of the ordinary retainers fleeing before the Dragon, which serves as a foil to Wiglaf's conduct by making it all the more exceptional: it is, indeed, of the same strain as Beowulf's.

A certain parallelism, moreover, subtly confirms that view. If the very recurrence of the words 'ealdsweord etonisc' in reference to Wiglaf's precious sword inherited from his father calls to mind the magic sword appearing in Grendel's lair, the parallel does not lead us very far. There is, however, in Wiglaf's attitude something rather akin to Beowulf's loyalty towards Hygelac (who was also his kinsman) as mentioned by him in his preceding speech. Beowulf stresses that he repaid his liege with his 'bright sword' (in battle) for what he had given him—and besides 'māðmas' there was 'lond' also ('eard ēðelwyn').[2] Now the main motivation of Wiglaf's heroic action is also the thought of what Beowulf had given him (especially the estate of the Wægmundings) which thought developed such an urge that 'ne mihte ðā forhabban.'[3] Thus both Beowulf and Wiglaf showed their gratitude towards their respective liege and benefactor in the true epic tradition. There is nothing remarkable, of course, in the parallelism, yet it reinforces the links which make of both heroes, the old King and the young retainer, men of the same cast—as of a common blood.

All this, however, has not given us an artistic justification for the digression on Weohstan. I am not sure whether it should not be sought for in the implications probably lurking behind the Swedish wars and the course which the Swedish-Geatish rivalry may have taken.

The main theme of this short digression is the story of Wiglaf's sword: how as Eanmund's heirloom it passed into the hands of Weohstan who killed him and brought it to Onela, and how Onela, though Eanmund was his brother's son, gave it as a present to Weohstan from whom Wiglaf inherited it on his

[1] *Beowulf*, ll. 2600–2601.   [2] *Ibid.*, ll. 2490–2493.   [3] *Ibid.*, l. 2609.

father's death. Now if we remember that the circumstances of
the Swedish wars were known by those for whom *Beowulf* was
composed, so that the poet might easily leave a certain number
of things as understood, we can draw an extremely important
conclusion. If Wiglaf's father, as 'lēod Scylfinga', had fought
on the side of Onela, the usurper, against his nephews Eanmund
and Eadgils, who had fled to the Geats (hereditary enemies of the
Swedes), the overthrow and death of Onela evidently carried
with it a complete reversal in Weohstan's position. Indeed, 'after
Ēadgils had been established on the throne, Wēohstān, who had
slain Ēanmund . . . was compelled to leave the country and
settled in the land of the Geats.'[1] The fact that Eadgils did not
apparently pursue him to avenge his brother's death is probably
due to his cordial relations with Beowulf who had assisted him
in his enterprise against Onela. Yet, and this is the first important
implication, was it likely that the slaying of Eanmund would be
definitely forgotten? Even if Weohstan had died, would not the
probable hostility of Eadgils be transferred to his son, together
with the famous sword, symbol of Weohstan's victory over
Eanmund?[2] If we remember that the mere aspect of some
'gomela lāfe', and particularly a sword, was enough to stir up
the latent enmity between Danes and Heathobards[3]—the sword
had become indeed the symbol of the triumph of one party over
the other—is it too adventurous to assume that the 'ealdsweord
etonisc' might probably be called to play a similar part in the
Swedish-Geatish feud? This would have been impossible as
long as Beowulf lived, but after his death, 'æfter hæleða hryre',
what then? Wiglaf himself was to ascend the Geatish throne
as heir and testamentary executor to Beowulf, and Wiglaf was
the son of Eanmund's 'bana'! Has not the emphasis on the
sword tremendous implications in such light?'[4]

Now should this interpretation seem to be lacking in a solid

---

[1] Klaeber, *Beowulf*, p. xliv.

[2] 'Kann man des Mörders nicht habhaft werden, so rächt man sich an seinem Sohn.
Die Sippe ist gleichsam eine Kollektivperson; den Schaden, den das einzelne Glied erleidet,
empfindet der ganze Körper, und daher ist es auch dem Rächer gleichgültig, welches Glied
er trifft, wenn er nur überhaupt Vergeltung üben kann' (J. Müller, *Das Kulturbild des
Beowulfepos*, Göttingen, 1914, pp. 21–22). See also the example of Wyðergyld's revenge in
the *Gesta Danorum*.

[3] See ll. 2032–2056.

[4] That the sword in question is supposed to have melted in the Dragon's blood does not
change much to the situation: it still remains, in the present digression, the symbol of the
probable enmity between Wiglaf and Eadgils which must have broken out shortly after
Beowulf's death.

basis, or too far-fetched, there is still another argument in support of it in our digression: the poet's comment on Onela's present to Weohstan. Onela gave him the sword, as we have just seen, 'þeah ðe hē his brōðor bearn ābredwade'; yet the actual pregnant words are these: 'nō ymbe ðā fæhðe spræc.'[1] What, I submit, the poet here leaves understood is that there came a time when that 'fæhðe' would not remain as tacit as on this occasion.[2] That Onela did not mention the feud was natural enough as he had usurped the throne and had himself undertaken an expedition against his nephews, the rightful heirs, who had fled to the Geats; in such circumstances he would not take any measures against Weohstan, who had assisted him in the fight, for having killed Eanmund! And yet 'herein is seen a breaking away from the primitive tribal custom'; and another critic explains Onela's 'passive attitude' by its being 'due to the fact that his nephew was a lawless exile, and so no longer entitled to protection from his kin.'[3] Eadgils, on the other hand, had certainly not Onela's reasons for assuming a passive attitude, and as a brother of Eanmund he probably waited for the first opportunity to speak 'ymbe ðā fæhðe'—in what words we may guess—and that opportunity would naturally have arisen with Beowulf's death, after Wiglaf's accession to the Geatish throne.

Finally what confirms these views is the celebrated foreboding of a future renewal of the feud between Geats and Swedes, and of the fall of the Geats, which looms so large towards the end of the poem. And this leads us to the last episode.

---

[1] *Beowulf*, ll. 2618–2619.

[2] This interpretation of what underlies the allusion to Wiglaf's sword, though, of course, conjectural, seems to us more likely than Mr. Du Bois's (which, by the way, does not exclude it), who connects the sword with his particular explanation of the Dragon and the Dragon fight. 'Since Beowulf represents the Geats as they are united and since the dragon represents them as they are divided Beowulf cannot rely only upon his own strength, the strength of thirty men—he is fighting against himself, and has to use a Swedish sword!' (Du Bois, *op. cit.*, p. 389). An objection against that view is that there is another glaring instance of a fight in which Beowulf is unable either to rely on his own strength, or 'þritiges manna mægencræft', a terrible struggle in which the hero can really not be said to fight against himself! The most dramatic moment in Beowulf's fight against Grendel's mother is indeed when the hero, after throwing away his useless sword, struggles with his arm's strength ('strenge getruwode, mundgripe mægenes'l 1533–1534), only to be overthrown by the fearful monster's assault. To escape final defeat he has to use a 'foreign' sword, the miraculous 'ealdsweord eotonisc' with which God provides him at the very last moment. Of course, in the fight against Grendel's dam, Beowulf is alone, whereas he is assisted towards the end of the Dragon fight by Wiglaf. Yet the presence of Wiglaf is justified by other more weighty reasons than an implied suggestion that by using a Swedish sword Beowulf is also fighting against himself.

[3] Seebohm, quoted by Klaeber, *Beowulf*, pp. 217–218. For the preceding quotaton, see *bid.*, *loc. cit.*

9. HYGELAC'S FALL; THE BATTLE AT RAVENSWOOD IN THE EARLIER SWEDISH WAR (2910–3007)

Wiglaf's messenger intimates that troublesome days are in store for the Geats when the Franks and Frisians hear of Beowulf's death. The Swedes are not to be trusted either. He then refers to the Geatish invàsion of Sweden (under Hæthcyn and Hygelac): 'though at first successful (even Ongenþēow's queen is taken prisoner), [it] seems destined to utter failure; the "old, terrible" king of the Swedes falls upon Hæðcyn's army, rescues the queen, kills the Geat king and forces his troops to seek refuge in the woods (*Hrefnesholt* 2935), threatening them all night long with death in the morning by the sword and the gallows. But at dawn the valorous Hygelāc appears with his division and inspires such a terror that the Swedes flee to their fastness, pursued by the Geats. Ongenþēow in a brave fight against two brothers, Eofor and Wulf, loses his life. Hygelāc, now king of the Geats, after his homecoming richly repaid the brothers and gave his only daughter as wife to Eofor.' [Klaeber, *Beowulf*, p. xxxix]. Such was the origin of the feud and enmity which the Swedes—so the messenger pursues—are likely to remember when they hear that Beowulf is dead.

(2910–3007)

This last digression deals with the actual origin of the Swedish-Geatish feud and depicts the first phase of the war between the two rival peoples. Of the four digressions dealing with the Swedish wars it is the longest and most detailed. What gives it its special interest, moreover, is the anticipations opening and concluding it, which now retrospectively justify the recurring allusions to the Swedish wars in the preceding episodes. It is only now that the whole effect of that haunting theme can be fully realized.

With the opening of that last digression the poet allows us for the first time to catch a glimpse of what the future has in store for the Geatish nation. The moment is particularly well chosen: it coincides with the announcement made to the Geats of Beowulf's death. The poet puts into the mouth of the messenger bringing the sorrowful tidings words of sinister purport which made of him a 'prophet of evil'. Now that the king has fallen, a time of war is to be expected—when the news has spread to the Francs and Frisians. Since Hygelac's raid—which is briefly recalled—the enmity between Franks and Geats has remained. Neither is any faith or friendship to be expected from the Swedes[1] —and then the dramatic phases of the first Swedish war are described.

The reference to the Frisian feud is skilful here in so far as it serves to emphasize, in a short parallel, the actual significance of the Swedish feud. If the Frisians, who after all repulsed Hygelac's attack with the aid of the Franks, defeating and killing him, are likely to remember this act of enmity and wage war on the Geats as soon as the fall of Beowulf provides them with a favourable opportunity (this is clearly to be understood from the messenger's allusions), how much more eager must be the Swedes to avail themselves of the opportunity, the Swedes who had been beaten and whose venerable king had been felled by the Geats! And here the description of the original feud, of the first war and Ongentheow's death, is singularly pertinent. This gives a considerable weight to the concluding words of the episode, hinting (more clearly even than in the case of the Frisians) at a future invasion on the part of the Swedes and leading finally to the crowning piece of epic prophecy.

It is not without any serious ground, indeed, that the story of Ongentheow's fall in the first Swedish war has been reserved for the last episode. The lack of chronological order needs an explanation. In reference to this Hoops writes: 'Es ist beachtenswert, dass der Bote bei seinen Prophezeiungen von neuen Kriegszügen der Schweden an die älteren Kämpfe zwischen Hygelac und Ongentheow anknüpft und die späteren zwischen Heardred und Onela ganz übergeht. Das hängt natürlich damit zusammen, dass der Dichter über diese schon früher (2379–96) berichtet hatte.'[2] This is quite right, and yet the real problem is not solved by what is merely an observation: we might well put the question in another way and ask why, then, has the war with Onela been treated before and not after the war against Ongentheow, according to the chronological order?

Let us first observe that there was no absolute necessity for the poet to follow the chronological order here, were it only for the simple reason that a knowledge of the historical events underlying these episodes could certainly be assumed on the part

---

[1] Such a conspicuous litotes (as well as the understatement concerning Frankish-Geatish enmity, ll. 2920–2921) is particularly significant here.
[2] Hoops, *Kommentar*, p. 310.

of those for whom *Beowulf* was intended. Any idea of a confusion
arising in their minds as to the natural sequence of those events
could be excluded. The poet was entirely at liberty, therefore, to
choose whatever order he found the most suitable or effective
for his purpose. Now the main object of the great episode
which leads from the Frisian expedition to the second Swedish
wars being the glorification of Beowulf, the poet naturally chose
a phase of the war in which Beowulf could play, and actually
played, a part. Onela's prudent attitude towards Beowulf, as
well as Beowulf's assistance to Eadgils are indirect testimonies
of the hero's might. It is quite natural, therefore, that the poet
did not want to miss utilizing those events that followed Hygelac's death, simply because he was going to refer, later on, to
earlier events connected with Hygelac's life. On the other hand
the events leading to Ongentheow's death, as they are presented
by the poet, offer some undeniable advantages. The first one—
if we remember that the poet wanted to stress how deep went the
roots of Swedish-Geatish enmity—is that the dramatic fights in
which first the Geats and then the Swedes lost their rulers were
not only the origin of the rivalry but a striking example of sheer
Swedish-Geatish feud. So much can hardly be said of the
conflict with Onela which was first and foremost a Swedish
civil war, involving a problem of disputed succession—a civil
war in which the Geats took part almost incidentally. The former
conflict was indeed more representative and, as a basis on which
a renewal of the strife could be prophesied, all the more effective.

It is, moreover, another example of the poet's method of
cross-reference which so often implies an effect of contrast: the
poet here subtly sets forth the first phase of the Swedish-Geatish
feud at the moment when he intimates the imminent opening of
the last phase; and if the first phase ended with a victory of the
Geats, the sombre forebodings at the close of the messenger's
speech definitely point to a Geatish defeat in the last—a defeat
probably amounting to practical annihilation.[1]

The choice, then, of the first Swedish-Geatish war at this point
in the poem is artistically justified and indirectly renders the
whole effect of the epic prophecy even more striking. The
picture of that threatening background in Geatish history is

---

[1] Indeed, 'the artistic effect of that catastrophe was carefully calculated'; though it
must be owned that 'it was an effect imposed upon the poet by historic facts that were too
well known to be tampered with' (Lawrence, *op. cit.*, p. 101) the way in which that effect was
used once more illustrates the high artistic sense of the *Beowulf* poet.

thus complete; the recurrent allusions which seemed not to be directly linked together, are now all of a sudden moulded into a vivid whole;[1] as we shall once more stress, from the moment the theme of the Swedish-Geatish rivalry has been introduced, there is no episode in the poem that does not deal with the Swedish wars. This haunting theme has now found its climax in the announcement of an imminent renewal of the feud, ending— 'æfter hæleða hryre'—in the fall of the Geats. This is one of the most dramatic points in the poem, as to the atmosphere at least. The epic prophecy, fraught with an oppressive melancholy, represents at its apex one of the essential and basic moods of the poem: the conclusion that all is transient in this worldly life. The sounds of the harp will die and give way to the croaks of the dark Raven, revelling over the 'wæl'—if ever there was indeed a prophet and a thing of evil, it is that 'wonna hrefn'!

In conclusion we shall say that the more important point which comes out clearly at the end of this first inquiry is this: though the subject-matter of this group of episodes—bearing as it does either on Beowulf himself or on the history of his own people— might by itself alone offer a sufficient degree of relevance to the main story and its background to justify their introduction into the poem, they are actually made to play, in addition to this, a significant and often quite subtle part in the organic structure of the poem. Skilfully using these episodes as a medium to convey certain impressions, the poet succeeds in reaching an artistic effect that generally transcends their immediate and tangible contents, and this by creating subtle links of relevance which are mostly suggested by means of delicate hints and very light touches rather than fully expressed and explicit statements.

Keeping in mind this important result, it will be interesting to see whether that group of episodes, the subject-matter of which is much more remote from the main story and its background, also provides similar traces of such a high artistic sense.

---

[1] We therefore suggest that Klaeber's statement as to the 'grave structural defects characteristic of the "Dragon Fight" ' (Klaeber, *Beowulf*, p. cvi), should be qualified. Artistically the structure of the Dragon part, far from being incoherent, has a higher unity of its own.

III. HISTORICAL, OR LEGENDARY, DIGRESSIONS NOT CONNECTED WITH BEOWULF AND THE GEATS

It is evident that if, owing to their narrative content, the episodes of this group are not directly connected with Beowulf or the history of his own people, they must have been introduced into the poem either for their own sake—because the poet, wanting a wider background to his story, incidentally drew on material which he thought fit to fascinate his audience—and this probably at the expense of the structural unity of the poem. Or, because the poet wanted to achieve through them a certain effect that might contribute to the artistic value of the poem. In this case we can justify their presence at the very place in which they figure in the main narrative.

1. THE FATE OF HEOROT (82–85)

The first of these episodes, though it hardly deserves that rather portentous term, is little more than a brief, incidental, allusion, a mere three and a half lines: the hall that Hrothgar had built stood 'high and wide-gabled' and the poet adds—

> 'heaðowylma bād,
> lāðan līges; ne wæs hit lenge þā gēn,
> þæt se ecghete āþumswēoran
> æfter wælnīðe wæcnan scolde.'
>
> (82–85)

Yet its interest has not escaped the eyes of the critics. Of course, the main subject of the discussion was to determine at what time, or at least on what occasion, the actual burning of the Hall occurred; and here, as on so many points touching the historical background of the poem, unanimity of opinion has not been attained. Though we are inclined to share Klaeber's view, who puts it in the Heathobards conflict,[1] we may safely regard this point as immaterial for an artistic interpretation of the digression.

The statement that the Hall was to be burned is enough to reach the intended effect. The very fact that the poet refers to

---

[1] Klaeber, *Beowulf*, pp. 129-130.

its disastrous end precisely at the moment in which he tells us of its construction and unsurpassed splendour is the first obvious instance in the poem of one of the author's favourite devices. The contrast inherent in the sudden *rapprochement* between a brilliant thing or harmonious situation vividly set forth and a brief intimation of disaster adds, in an effective way, to the impression of melancholy and sadness in which so much of the poem is steeped.

Another instance is the allusion to the 'Brosinga mene' (digression of Eormenric and Hama), of which we have already spoken in connection with the first reference to Hygelac's fateful expedition.[1] We shall merely point out—to add a few comments on that digression—that here again, in order to appreciate the value of the digression in the poem, there is no need to reconstruct the original story, of which so many points still remain in the dark. Just as Heorot was a paragon, the 'Brosinga mene' was reputed to be one of the most marvellous jewels on earth. Yet behind so much splendour looms again disaster: Hama stole it away when fleeing from the 'crafty enmity' ('searonīðas flēah')[2] of tyrannous Eormenric. And even if there is no allusion to Hama's death, as was formerly thought,[3] one point at least is sure: it passed to Hygelac who had it when he fell on Frisian ground where it was stolen by 'wyrsan wīg-frecan' plundering the corpses of the Geats.[4] What is characteristic here is that of all the allusions to Hygelac's end this is the only one that stresses its disastrous aspect alone, and not without definite reason. To our mind, therefore, the allusion to the 'Brosinga mene' cannot be separated from the reference to Hygelac's raid with which it here forms a digressional unit.

It might be added that modern descendants of the 'Brosinga mene' are to be found in those fantastic stories of celebrated diamonds which are supposed to be fatal to their successive

---

[1] pp. 23–24.
[2] *Beowulf*, l. 1200.
[3] As is known, 'gecēas ēcne rǣd' (1201) was interpreted as 'died'. Though this view is now generally abandoned (see Klaeber, *Beowulf*, p. 179; Hoops, *Kommentar*, pp. 150–151) it is quite satisfactory from an artistic point of view and might be conveniently retained. It is still adopted, as a matter of fact, both by Professor Sedgefield, who thinks that 'surely it can only mean "entered upon the eternal way," i.e. died' (W. J. Sedgefield, ed., *Beowulf*, 3rd ed., Manchester, 1935, p. 123) and by Prof. K. Malone (*English Studies*, XV, 151). That behind the 'wonderfully precious' jewel lurks the death of Hama who carried it away is just the kind of irony which might be expected here.
[4] *Beowulf*, l. 1212.

owners, and the 'career' of which is teeming with theft, murder, and further drama of the most lamentable sort!

More important still are the forebodings of family strife among the Danes alluded to precisely at the moment in which the present harmony at the King's court is emphasized. An element of contrast which is conspicuous again in the Ingeld-Freawaru passage.[1] Finally, the forebodings of the fall of the Geats—the crowning piece in that gloomy series of sinister hints—are likewise brought into relief by the digression that comes just before, which calls to mind a glorious phase of early Geatish history.[2]

At this point the impression of melancholy and sadness is felt with such an intensity that it is almost an obsession. The poem could very well find its end there—and in some way it is already a kind of end. Yet, artistically, it could hardly close on such an oppressive mood; some attenuation was needed, and the details of Beowulf's obsequies—though the sombre implications are still there—certainly bring it. It could evidently be argued that the funeral had to take place anyway—of course, but the epic prophecy could also have been used as a closing scene, after the obsequies themselves. The present order has indeed its reasons. The poem can close on a certain note of appeasement with the last words in praise of the hero. Thanks to this, it is perhaps still felt, but with much less intensity, that the consequences of the hero's sacrifice which was meant to save his own people, and in fact did . . . for a time, actually precipitated the disastrous epilogue closing the history of the now 'ealdorlēase' Geats.

2. STORIES OF SIGEMUND AND HEREMOD (871–915)

On the way back to Heorot the court poet improvises a lay in honour of Beowulf and compares him to Sigemund and Heremod. He mentions Sigemund's fights against the giants (undertaken in company with his nephew Fitela) and his success-ful dragon fight. Sigemund was indeed the most famous warrior since Heremod's death. Though he had raised great expectations, Heremod became cruel and tyrannous and was hated by the people, whereas everybody loves Beowulf.

(871–915)

---

[1] *Beowulf*, ll. 2062 ff.   [2] *Ibid.*, ll. 2910 ff.

The stories of Sigemund and Heremod, or rather their introduction into the poem, have been interpreted with great insight by Professor Hoops, whose views may be safely endorsed. In Klaeber's words, 'Hoops regards the entire passage as a summary of a single lay in praise of Bēowulf, of which the Sigemund and Heremod verses are integral parts.'[1] Klaeber does not say that he is ready to endorse Hoops's opinion, but one thing at least is obvious: whether considered as a single lay or as a juxtaposition of two improvised lays (as Klaeber seems to suggest), the whole digression is definitely intended to praise Beowulf.[2]

In fact it is given a definite unity by the two references to the Geatish hero, one introducing, the other concluding, the stories of Sigemund and Heremod. From the 'lay of praise concerning Beowulf's exploit', improvised in honour of the hero (the summary of which we are spared, as we have just been told the whole story), the court poet, as Klaeber finely remarks, 'proceeds to recite the adventures of Sigemund, thus raising Bēowulf, as it were, to the rank of pre-eminent Germanic heroes.'[3] This 'consecration', if we may say so, is indeed the main point of the digression.

The very choice of the heroes—out of many—is highly significant. Between Beowulf and both of them there is at the same time a parallelism and a contrast, partly implicit, partly explicit, and not devoid of a slight dramatic irony.

With Sigemund the parallelism resides, of course, in the Dragon adventure, and what adds to its dramatic quality is that, as the audience are aware of it, knowing as they do that Beowulf in his turn was to achieve 'dōm unlytel' by killing the Dragon, the scop's *rapprochement* was of much greater pertinence and significance than he himself and the Danes could have actually imagined. This is what might be called the anticipatory (and implicit) element in the parallel as opposed to the element constituted by the allusions to the killing of numerous monsters by Sigemund and his companion: 'hæfdon ealfela eotena cynnes sweordum gesǣged'.[4] The contrast between Sigemund and Beowulf, on the other hand, is that while the former survived the Dragon fight, the latter did not. That those who knew

[1] Klaeber, *Beowulf*, p. 158.
[2] *Ibid., loc. cit.* See also Bartlett, *op. cit.*, p. 21.
[3] Klaeber, *ibid.*   [4] *Beowulf*, ll. 883–884.

should not remain under the impression of the contrast (however light the touch) needed the introduction of a second parallel, that with Heremod.

Here the 'immediate' purpose of the parallel is the reference to Heremod's former strength and courage ('eafoð ond ellen')—in which he doubtless matched the greatest heroes—the anticipatory part is that his sorrowful end was not to be Beowulf's lot. At the same time the poet stresses the contrast (this time to Beowulf's great advantage) between Heremod's tyranny and the aversion it brought about, and Beowulf's popularity. With this contrast, which so effectively completes this hymn to Beowulf's greatness, the episode is at an end.[1]

As a conclusion we may consider the whole episode as being indeed a hymn in praise of Beowulf, to which both the court poet and the *Beowulf* poet contribute in a subtle way. It is well constructed, the transition between its four parts being both natural and, as Hoops remarks, unforced.[2] The Heremod allusion, therefore—which is an integral part of it and closes with a word of eulogy on Beowulf, as the counterpart of the word of praise preceding the Sigemund allusion—can hardly be considered as too widely digressional, as Klaeber suggests when he writes that 'when the Heremōd theme is taken up, we feel like questioning whether Hrōðgār's thane has not been altogether forgotten by the Ags. poet.'[3] It is, to say the least, significant that the poet was so satisfied with the Heremod-Beowulf contrast and found it so effective that he used it a second time and made a third and brief allusion to it in the course of the poem.

3. HEREMOD'S TRAGEDY (1709–1722)

This second Heremod digression serves as a kind of exordium to Hrothgar's great 'twenty parson power' speech.

'Ne wearð Heremōd swā
eaforum Ecgwelan, Ār-Scyldingum;
ne gewēox hē him tō willan, ac tō wælfealle
ond tō dēaðcwalum Deniga lēodum;

---

[1] There is, furthermore, another parallelism in the fact that 'Sigemund, Heremod, and possibly Finn were the last great representatives of great houses, akin in that respect to Hroþgar, Hygelac and Beowulf' (Du Bois, *op. cit.*, p. 379; on the dramatic irony implied in the allusion to Sigemund's dragon fight, see *ibid.*, p. 380).

[2] Hoops, *Beowulfstudien*, p. 54.

[3] Klaeber, *Beowulf*, p. 158.

> brēat bolgenmōd bēodgenēatas,
> eaxlgesteallan, oþ þæt hē āna hwearf,
> mǣre þēoden mondrēamum from,
> ðēah þe hine mihtig God mægenes wynnum,
> eafeþum stēpte, ofer ealle men
> forð gefremede. Hwæþere him on ferhþe grēow
> brēosthord blōdrēow; nallas bēagas geaf
> Denum æfter dōme; drēamlēas gebād,
> þæt hē þæs gewinnes weorc þrōwade,
> lēodbealo longsum.'

(1709–1722)

It is not the place here to discuss at great length the speech as a whole, and to examine whether it should be regarded as a later addition or not. Yet it can be said that within the speech, and as its first main object, the new Heremod digression is perfectly apposite. Just as the story of Cresus afforded an eminently suitable 'exemplum' to many a moralist, so the story of Heremod 'exalted at one time over all men, and then deposed, and sent into exile in misery and disgrace . . . afforded moralists like Hrothgar an alluring theme.'[1] To show the dangers of 'arrogance and greed in a king', a point on which Hrothgar, addressing Beowulf as a future ruler, wanted to insist, a better illustration could hardly have been chosen. The implication is that Beowulf is now practically as mighty and glorious as Heremod at the height of his career (who was also 'strongest of mankind'), but that he has yet to show greater moral qualities than Heremod to escape a similar disastrous reversal. It is on such qualities that Hrothgar insists, and such he, of course, expects from Beowulf. The last allusion to Heremod in the poem will show how much they were indeed fulfilled by Beowulf.

Within the poem also (and this makes it necessary to dwell on the purpose of the speech in the structure of the poem) the episode is likewise perfectly apposite. We must first insist on an aspect of the speech which does not seem to have so far attracted sufficient attention on the part of the critics. If we are not mistaken, at least one of the main objects of the old king's speech is to serve as a subtle transition between the two great divisions of the epic, the Grendel part and the Dragon part. The fact that

---

[1] Lawrence, *Beowulf and Epic Tradition*, p. 84.

E

Hrothgar, who is well placed as an aged king, full of experience and knowledge, a kind of Nordic Nestor,[1] to administer moral advice, makes of the 'métier de roi' the main theme of his farewell speech to Beowulf suggests that it is a kind of preparation and prologue to Beowulf's future career as a king. Up to now Beowulf was only 'Hygelac's thane', and now he suddenly grows into a potential ruler. The speech suggests that Beowulf is precisely to be faced with the problem of which Heremod presents the main aspect: how to make use of his power at the moment when God exalts him over all other men. Heremod's example, whom God 'ofer ealle men forð gefremede'[2] is but a classical illustration of how a flaw may bring to nought even great qualities, and how dangerous greatness is if *not* accompanied by magnanimity and modesty (submission to God). Why should this be said to Beowulf if not to be of use to him, once he was in similar circumstances?[3]

Hrothgar's admonition is, indeed, the direct sign and premonition of the career that awaits Beowulf, and therefore leads to, and provides a powerful link with, the second part of the poem.[4]

---

[1] The parallel with Nestor is already in Schücking (see *Heldenstolz*, p. 32).

[2] *Beowulf*, ll. 1717b–1718a.

[3] That this passage of Hrothgar's 'sermon' is a reference to 'the part he [Beowulf] is to play as a king of the Geats' is also Miss Blomfield's opinion (*op. cit.*, p. 401).

[4] This explanation differs widely from Mr. Du Bois's, who sees in Hrothgar's words an actual prophecy hinting at future defects in Beowulf. 'Hroþgar warns Beowulf against proud overconfidence and the unexpected approach of the enemy by night and against sloth and the consequent non-distribution of rings and loss of heroic character. During the early part of his career Beowulf aided the Danes, fought with Hygelac against the Franks, and avenged Heardred upon Onela. But the latter part of that career appears to have been passed inactively till the surprise attack of the dragon roused Geatland, and the effect of this luxurious inactivity, answering Hroþgar's prophecies, is evident in the fact that a base fellow first surprises the Geats by discovering the dragon and that Beowulf's berserkers turn cowardly at a critical moment' (Du Bois, *op. cit.*, p. 401).

That Beowulf's escort does not stand the supreme trial and flees at the appearance of the monster needs no such explanation; this motive, which is frequent in heroic actions of the kind, serves as a foil to enhance the exceptional character of the hero's courage and resolution. Moreover, 'it throws the strongest light upon the heroism of the single faithful retainer' (Lawrence, *op. cit.*, p. 228). Though the discovery of the hoard and the theft of a precious cup belonging to it by a 'base fellow', as well as Beowulf's absence from his home at the time of the dragon's first attack, are more difficult to explain, they do not necessarily point to a possible period of sloth or weakness on the part of the hero. We think, on the contrary, that Beowulf actually avoided the dangers against which Hrothgar warned him, and applied his precepts to the uttermost. The very point lies in the fact that having now equalled Heremod at the apex of his career and fame, Beowulf is going to prove greater than Heremod and avoid his lamentable fall; this by exhibiting precisely the moral qualities which Heremod so obviously lacked.

These qualities are first and foremost modesty, kindness and generosity, as opposed to Heremod's arrogance ('oferhygde', leading to tyranny) and avarice ('nallas beagas geaf', 1719). If Hrothgar's words were prophetic of a future weakness in Beowulf (instead of

The speech makes us actually feel, before the event itself, that we are about to enter on an important new turn in our hero's life—and this has been so skilfully done that the explicit transition itself could be condensed into a few lines: this turning point had already been hinted at and prepared![1]

The explicit transition, moreover, is preceded by a last and brief allusion to Heremod,[2] which delicately reminds us of Hrothgar's admonition, and is therefore a last link between the

being a touchstone by which his actual greatness can be measured) what would be the point of the later eulogy:

> nealles druncne slōg
> heorðgenēatas; næs him hrēoh sefa,
> ac hē mancynnes mǣste cræfte
> ginfæstan gife, þē him God sealde,
> hēold hildedēor.   (2179b–2183a)

in which he is once more implicitly contrasted to Heremod by means of these striking litotes? And even if it should be argued that Beowulf's weakness appears later, what would be the point of Beowulf's own retrospective survey of the 'creditable facts of his life' when, as a dying man, he is prepared to meet the Lord:

> Ic ðās lēode hēold
> fīftig wintra; næs sē folccyning,
> ymbesittendra ǣnig ðāra,
> þē mec gūðwinum grētan dorste,
> egesan ðēon. Ic on earde bād
> mǣlgesceafta, hēold mīn tela,
> ne sōhte searoniðas, nē mē swōr fela
> āða on unriht. Ic ðæs ealles mæg
> feorhbennum sēoc gefēan habban;
> forðām mē wītan ne ðearf Waldend fīra
> morðorbealo māga, þonne mīn sceaceð
> līf of līce.   (2732b–2743a)

Those words inevitably remind us of the Heremod contrast. They are no mere 'gylp', and show how, in fact, Beowulf proved true to the ideal once set forth by Hrothgar! If part of Beowulf's career had been spent in 'luxurious inactivity' and sloth, would the poet have insisted on the fact that no enemy ever dared to attack or even threaten him? Finally, to complete and confirm the characterization of the hero on the lines given by the contrast with Heremod, we have the poet's ultimate judgment mentioning Beowulf as 'manna mildust ond mon(ðw)ǣrust' (3181). As Mr. Batchelor puts it, 'the moral of the poem . . . is that Bēowulf deeply impressed all whom he met, even the truculent Unferth, as being the kindest and mildest of chieftains' (C. C. Batchelor, 'The Style of the "Beowulf": A Study of the Composition of the Poem', *Speculum*, XII, July 1937, p. 340). This final judgment, which gives us in an epitome (and as an epitaph) Beowulf's most characteristic moral trait throughout his career, cannot be dismissed as conventional praise: it is, on the contrary, his moral greatness as well as his physical strength which put Beowulf above all men.

The fact that Beowulf is to go farther than Hrothgar in the ideal of kingship is shown in the implicit contrast between Hrothgar's attitude towards Grendel, which is mainly passive—though Hrothgar had otherwise been so great a protector to his people (see especially ll. 1769–1773)—and Beowulf's attitude towards the dragon leading to the hero's supreme sacrifice. This contrast is certainly meant to give us the real measure of Beowulf's greatness, and not a measure of Hrothgar's weakness!

This implicit contrast, moreover, is another link between the Grendel and the Dragon parts—just as Hrothgar's sermon serves as a significant transition between them.

[1] This likewise explains that, apart from that transition, 'only a hint of Bēowulf's future kingship is vouchsafed after the second victory, 1850 ff.' (Klaeber, *Beowulf*, p. li).

[2] *Beowulf*, ll. 2180 ff.

first part of Beowulf's life, his adventures in Denmark, and his career as a king.[1] That in the Dragon part of the poem the hero more than fulfils the highest duties expected from an ideal sovereign eventually gives the true measure of Beowulf's greatness. Indeed, I am not sure whether we should not perhaps add to the significant contrast pointed out by critics in reference to the Danish part,[2] between Hrothgar the hoary king, and young Beowulf, a contrast between Hrothgar, an embodiment and picture of a king, and Beowulf's own figure as a ruler in the Dragon part.

In a way Hrothgar embodies an ideal of kingship which, as has been shown by Professor Schücking, is closely akin to the Augustinian ideal of the *imperator felix*.[3] In his great speech he draws that picture of an ideal ruler in opposition to Heremod's failure. The so-called 'sermon' is only a sort of edifying comment, on a more general scale, upon the lesson drawn from the Heremod illustration. Moralization not being as a rule, even in those times, a synonym for brevity, we should not wonder at the relative length of the 'sermon'. That it is closely connected with (nay, a sort of moralizing epilogue to) the Heremod episode is shown by its conclusion, a renewed exhortation not to submit to such sins as led to Heremod's fall: 'Bebeorh þē ðone bealoniðˀ, ... oferhȳda ne gȳm, mǣre cempa!'[4]

Now the striking point is that Beowulf (who also presents from the outset characteristic traits of the same Augustinian ideal), once in the position of a king, actually transcends by far this picture of an ideal king with the ultimate sacrifice of his own life in favour of his people, the significance of which is stressed by the very contrast with Hrothgar's own attitude towards

[1] The reference to Beowulf's accession to the Geatish throne comes but some twenty-five lines later (see ll. 2206 ff.).

[2] 'Was ihm [the poet] im ersten Teil des Epos vorschwebt, wenn er Hroðgar und Beowulf zusammenführt, das ist wohl in erster Linie, den alten Mann von dem in der Fülle seiner Kraft stehenden zu unterscheiden' (Schücking, *Heldenstolz*, p. 31).
Professor Tolkien likewise considers that the chief purpose of the first section is the 'direct contrast of youth and age in the persons of Beowulf and Hrothgar' (J. R. R. Tolkien, *Beowulf, The Monsters and the Critics*, London, 1936, p. 31).

[3] See L. L. Schücking, *Königsideal*, p. 146. 'Der Fürst muss Herr über seine Begierden und Leidenschaften sein, besonders der grössten und für ihn gefährlichsten Sünde, dem Hochmut (superbia) nicht Gewalt über sich gönnen, sondern bescheiden und demütig bleiben. Sein Herrschen sei ein Dienen, in Liebe, Wo(h)lwollen, mitleidiger Fürsorge.' (Cf. also *ibid.*, p. 148.)

[4] *Beowulf*, ll. 1758, 1760–1761. Mr. Whitbread sees a possibility of justifying the 'inordinate length of Hroðgar's speech' by assuming that it followed 'a set rhetorical pattern' similar to that of *Deor* (L. Whitbread, 'Beowulfiana', *Modern Language Review*, XXXVII, October, 1942, pp. 482–483).

Grendel. Yet Hrothgar was already the figure of an ideal king! No wonder Klaeber was led to suppose that when describing the character of Beowulf as a leader, the poet 'was almost inevitably reminded of the Saviour, the self-sacrificing King, the prototype of supreme perfection'[1]!

4. THE STORY OF MODTHRYTHO,[2] THE WIFE OF OFFA (1931–1962)

Beowulf returns to Geatland with his comrades. They have landed safely and are on their way to the kingly hall where Hygelac resides with his young wife Hygd. Though she has reigned but a for a few years, she has proved a generous queen. Modthrytho—and here the digression abruptly begins—perpetrated terrible deeds. No man dared look at her because he knew that if he did he would soon be put to death. 'Ne bið swylc cwēnlīc þēaw idese tō efnanne,' the poet says. On her father's bidding she sailed to the court of Offa and no sooner had she married him than she gave up her violent ways, and became a generous queen at Offa's side, who was himself a brave and excellent ruler. They had a son called Eomer.

(1931–1962)

If the Heremod digression is thus closely connected with the problem of leadership, one aspect at least of the Offa digression might also be related to the same problem. But more of this later on.

Of all the historical digressions this is apparently the least apposite in the poem—'far fetched and out of place as it seems', writes Klaeber[3]—and it may have been introduced for the sake of its containing a topical reference. Attempts have been made to disentangle the exact point underlying the use of the story. The best known of these is Earle's tentative explanation that the allusion involves 'a poetic and veiled admonition addressed to Cynethryth.' But this has been refuted by Chambers, who also shows that we have not the slightest reason to believe that the episode is a later interpolation (which might have removed the

---

[1] Klaeber, *Beowulf*, p. cxxi.
[2] As Klaeber concludes: 'the reading *Mōdþrȳðo*, although not certain beyond dispute, seems the best that could be adopted under the trying circumstances' (*ibid.*, p. 199).
[3] *Ibid.*, p. cvii.

chronological difficulty of an allusion to Cynethryth).[1] We must be content to say that in all probability the poet 'was interested in the old Anglian traditions',[2] without making any pronouncement as to his reasons for such an interest. That is indeed the only conclusion which, according to Klaeber, can reasonably be drawn from that much discussed episode.

Here again, however, we shall try and apply the artistic criterion. The point which concerns us is this: even supposing there were excellent topical reasons—though unknown to us—for introducing the digression into the poem; either it was introduced, then, for these reasons only, and the digression is likely to be of no value at all in the structure of the poem (this might favour the assumption of an interpolation). Or the poet was enough of an artist not to subordinate his episode entirely to its topical value, but to give it at the same time its function, however slight, in the organization of the poem. In this case, the theory of an interpolation, though not excluded, becomes quite unnecessary.

In the first place, the way in which the episode is introduced is again typical of the *Beowulf* poet and once more displays the favourite device of contrast. This, of course, has been pointed out by critics. As Professor Sedgefield writes, 'there is clearly a contrast intended by the poet between the young and gracious Hygd and a certain queen of story of a criminally violent temper. We may compare the contrast drawn in ll. 1709 ff. and ll. 901 ff. between Beowulf and Heremod.'[3] No doubt about this, and the comparison with the Beowulf-Heremod parallel is quite pertinent: Modthrytho is evidently conceived as a foil to the young queen, Hygd. Yet the similarity of the device is not enough to justify the introduction of the episode from the aesthetic point of view: one feels that it is somewhat disproportionate to the simple result of affording a foil, however effective, to Hygd's qualities. The connecting link with the rest of the poem would decidedly be too tenuous, which is obviously not the case with the Beowulf-Heremod contrast. There is, however,

---

[1] See Chambers, *Introduction*, pp. 37–38.
[2] Klaeber, *Beowulf*, p. 198.
[3] W. J. Sedgefield, *Beowulf*, ed. cit., p. 130. See likewise Blomfield, *op. cit.*, p. 401: 'In accordance with the filling and deepening of the courtly scenes in this part, a disquisition on the ideal type of high-born lady, shown by contrast with Þryðo just as the ideal king is contrasted with Heremod, is attached to the person of Hygd.'

a link which confers a definite relevance to this episode and it must precisely be sought in its connection with the preceding episode concerning Heremod.

Apart from the twofold contrast between Beowulf and Heremod, and between Modthrytho and Hygd (which is a parallelism in the device merely), we can detect a further contrast subtly connecting Heremod himself and Modthrytho. If we compare the respective careers of Heremod and Modthrytho, it immediately appears that they ran an exactly opposite course. Whereas Heremod, endowed with great qualities, had distinguished himself above all men, and consequently awoke the highest expectations—yet ended lamentably because he abused his power and became cruel to his subjects, Modthrytho began as a cruel and tyrannous princess (a feminine Heremod at his worst), shedding the blood of many a retainer—yet 'redeeming time when men thought least she would' once on the Anglian throne at Offa's side became renowned for her goodness! This striking opposition thus provides a connecting link between the Heremod and the Modthrytho-Offa episode.

At the same time it again stresses the problem of the 'use of power.' Heremod's failure after such brilliant promise and Modthrytho's success after the worst beginnings are themselves implicitly contrasted with Offa, whose whole career was a long and continuous success and who, therefore, in the poet's brief and condensed eulogy, may give us a kind of prefiguration of Beowulf's own future successful leadership. From this standpoint the Modthrytho-Offa episode completes—though in a less visible way, we must admit—the part played by the Heremod allusions, and is thus more than a purely topical digression.[1] The assumption that the episode is a later interpolation becomes practically useless, and the artistic criterion confirms what the use of the device as well as the moralizing tone already suggested, namely that the passage may be considered as truly Beowulfian.

[1] If the poet were merely throwing a dart at some contemporary queen 'of a neighbouring and hostile kingdom' (see Lawrence, *Beowulf and Epic Tradition,* p. 277) why did he not stop, then, after the allusion to Modthrytho's shrewishness, 'the whole point of the episode', instead of continuing up to her marriage with Offa and her reformation? In our assumption the reformation of Modthrytho is accounted for by its contrast to Heremod's career. That the contrast seems too far-fetched is an objection which can be met by pointing to the fact that the contrast between Hygd and Modthrytho almost immediately called into mind (not only with the critics who have pointed it out but with the general reader) the parallel contrast between Beowulf and Heremod.

5. THE FINN AND HEATHOBARDS EPISODES (1066–1159; 2024–2069)

The Finn Episode. In the course of a brilliant ceremony at Heorot in honour of Beowulf's victory, the hero has been offered rich presents by the King. The festivities are carried on and then the court poet recites the Tale of Finnsburg. We here give Klaeber's brief summary of the Finn legend:

'A band of sixty Danes under their chief Hnæf find themselves attacked before daybreak in the hall of the Frisian King Finn, whom they have come to visit. . . . Five days they fight without loss against the Frisians, but (here the Episode sets in) at the end Hnæf and many of his men, as well as of the Frisians, are counted among the dead. In this state of exhaustion Finn concludes a treaty with Hengest, who has assumed command over the Danes. The fallen warriors of both tribes are burned together amid appropriate ceremonies. Hengest with his men stays in Friesland during the winter. But deep in his heart burns the thought of revenge. The day of reckoning comes when the Danes Gūðlāf and Oslāf, unable to keep any longer the silence imposed upon them by the terms of the treaty, openly rebuke their old foes. Finn is set upon and slain, and Hildeburh together with the royal treasure of the Frisians carried home to the land of the Danes' (Klaeber, *Beowulf*, pp. 231–32).
(1066–1159)

The Ingeld Episode. In his report to Hygelac Beowulf describes his reception at Heorot and alludes to the king's daughter Freawaru, who distributed the ale-cups to the 'duguðe'.

The young princess is engaged to Froda's son (Ingeld). The match was destined to put an end to the endless feud between Danes and Heathobards. Beowulf then intimates that such a settlement is bound to be transient: the followers of Freawaru will carry swords that once belonged to Heathobard warriors who had been killed in battle (by the Danes), and the Heathobards will resent it. Then an 'old grim warrior, chafing under the trying situation' and remembering the death of those men, incites a young comrade, whose father's sword is now carried by a Dane in the hall of the Heathobards, to an act of revenge. Again and again he spurs him on with bitter words until the young man kills Freawaru's thane. Retaliation will follow on the part of the Danes and this will kindle Ingeld's 'wælnīðas' whereas his love for his wife will grow cold. Therefore, concludes Beowulf,

> 'ic Heaðo-Bear[d]na hyldo ne telge,
> dryhtsibbe dæl Denum unfæcne,
> frēondscipe fæstne.'

(2024–2069)

The most interesting glimpses we get of events underlying Danish history are no doubt the Finnsburg tale and the Heatho-bards episode: Both are characteristic by their dramatic intensity, and the latter is generally acknowledged one of the finest passages in the poem. Yet it is not so much their intrinsic qualities which we shall try to investigate as, again, their actual value in the organic structure of the poem.

What the themes of these two episodes imply can only be properly understood when viewed in connection with the Dragon part. To put it in other words, the Dragon part, or, to be more accurate, its background alone, can give the ultimate justification of the presence of these episodes in the poem viewed as an organic whole. They indirectly but palpably help to bring to its highest pitch the tragic keynote of that dramatic background. But let us first examine the dominating themes.

Speaking of the allusions to Danish history and the events to which they refer, Professor Klaeber writes: 'Thus the two tragic motives of this epic tradition are the implacable enmity between the two tribes, dominated by the idea of revenge which no human bonds of affection can restrain, and the struggle for the crown among members of a royal family.'[1] Whatever the divergences of critics concerning the reconstruction of the 'Finn legend', the one settled point which has never been open to doubt is indeed the central theme of the story, i.e., how the irresistible force of tribal enmity sooner or later sweeps aside with its imperative all human attempts at a compromise. This can best be realized if we compare the Finn episode with the 'Fragment'.

The 'Fight at Finnsburg' is, of course, of special interest as it presents an independent treatment of the Finn legend which allows us, by comparison, to catch a glimpse of the *Beowulf* poet

---

[1] Klaeber, *Beowulf*, p. xxxvi.

at work on one point at least of the poem. Critics have shown that there is a fair amount of agreement between the two versions,[1] especially if allowance is made for the fact that one is most probably an independent lay and the other an episode which had to be fitted into the context of a great epic poem. It is precisely the few divergences (or some of them at any rate) which are of an undoubted value for us. The most important of them, which has often been pointed out, is a characteristic shift of emphasis in the episode. The *Beowulf* poet passes 'over the matter of fighting . . . in the most cursory fashion',[2] whereas he dwells on the pathetic situation of Queen Hildeburh and on the spiritual conflict of Hengest—both being the outstanding figures of the Episodes. The treatment is thus more heroic in the Fragment, more 'sentimental' in the episode.

Now if the *Beowulf* poet thus stressed with obvious sympathy the human—one might even say psychological—element, it is not only because of its emotional appeal, which would naturally find an immediate response in an audience fond of such tragic situations; it is also because it considerably heightens the ultimate effect of the central theme. Could the elementary and irresistible force of the enmity between the two tribes be made more tangible and brought home to us in a more suggestive way than by the medium of such spiritual sufferings and conflicts? Hildeburh's distress vividly brings out the theme of the precarious peace, that even sacred human bonds are utterly unable to save.[3] And here we shall point out that the assumption that Hildeburh 'had been given in marriage to the Frisian chief in

---

[1] Concerning the details, a greater harmony between the Episode and the Fragment could be attained if the name 'Guðlafes' (l. 33 of the Fragment) were taken, as was suggested by Mr. Beaty in his study of echo-words, as a 'common noun which means war-survivor and is an echo of the Guðlaf, proper noun, in l. 16' (J. O. Beaty, 'The Echo-Word in "Beowulf" with a Note on the "Finnsburg Fragment,"' *Publications of the Modern Language Association of America*, XLIX, June 1934, p. 373).

[2] Klaeber, *Beowulf*, p. 236. 'Whereas the *Fragment* is inspired by the lust and joy of battle, the theme of the *Episode*, as told in *Beowulf*, is rather the pity of it all; the legacy of mourning and vengeance which is left to the survivors:
>   For never can true reconcilement grow
>   Where wounds of deadly hate have struck so deep.'
(Chambers, *Introduction*, p. 248.)

[3] The contrast between Hildeburh's innocence and the 'dark background of treachery' (which is, after all, one element of the theme of the precarious peace) has been finely thrown into light by Professor Malone: the poet 'is drawing for us a pathetic figure, a woman, innocent but helpless in the hands of an evil destiny. The poet protests for us. What had she done to bring upon herself such terrible suffering? And he answers, she was wholly without guilt. He thus contrasts, as strongly as he can, the background of treachery with the innocent figure who stands out in relief against it' (K. Malone, 'The Finn Episode in "Beowulf",' *Journal of English and Germanic Philology*, XXV, April 1926, p. 161).

the hope of securing permanent peace',[1] or, to put it in the poet's words, had been used as 'freoðuwebbe' seems to us extremely probable and satisfactory: in such a light the whole passage can only gain in dramatic force.

Hengest's dilemma and final resolve likewise brings out, and this time more directly, the theme of the precarious truce. However solemnly sworn and reasonable in its terms, the compact was doomed to be broken owing to the extraordinary power of the urge for vengeance. Two points are worth considering here. It is indeed on that point that the Episode again differs from the Fragment. Whereas the latter, in what has been called 'epic exaggeration',[2] reports that none of the defenders of the Hall were killed in the fight, the episode mentions, among others, the killing of Hnæf, the chief of the Danes himself. As Lawrence pointed out, the '*Episode* would have no point without the death of Hnæf and the obligation of vengeance, which motivate the entire tragic situation.'[3] The death of Hnæf is indeed of the greatest importance both in the 'Hildeburh part'—the unhappy queen thus losing her brother and her son who fought on opposite sides—and in the 'Hengest part', as it is the main reason for the breaking of the oath to Finn, the duty of revenge for the fallen chieftain having been ultimately put before the 'allegiance to an over-lord.' On the other hand, to be really so effective, the dilemma had to be made particularly hard to solve and consequently the compact had to appear as a deliberate and responsible compromise. The poet insisted, therefore, on this trait: honour had been saved by the terrible fight in such a way that unless they intended to fight on to a complete and reciprocal extermination—like the famous lions of the fable, of whom only the tails were left—they had to make a truce. And the very terms of the truce which is *offered* by Finn (and not asked by the Danes)—especially the clause concerning a possible taunt about the awkward situation of the Danes—certainly preserve in the utmost measure the honour of the Danes.[4] But (there is so often a 'but' after victories in

[1] Klaeber, *Beowulf*, p. 231.
[2] Lawrence, *Beowulf and Epic Tradition*, p. 119.
[3] Lawrence, *ibid.*
[4] After having enumerated the six clauses of the truce, Professor Malone points out 'that all these clauses represent concessions or promises on the part of Finn. Nothing is said about any obligations assumed by the Danes, and on the face of it, Hengest certainly drove a good bargain.' That we have to deal here with a deliberate purpose on our poet's part, entailing some definite exaggeration, is likewise clear: 'Finn is represented as entering

Beowulf) the greater this victory, which had its motivation in the very circumstances in which the *Episode* was recited,[1] the sharper the contrast with the 'clouds of future shadow' gathering behind the subtle allusions of the following scene. Here we enter upon a more speculative plane, without losing touch, however, with the reality of the text—and in the protecting shadow of an authoritative critic.

As soon as the Finnsburg lay has been sung, convivial mirth rises again and suddenly the whole attention is focussed on Queen Wealhtheow, who is about to address Beowulf. Before she has even uttered a word, in the very brief picture of the scene in the hall—and five lines only after the last words of the Finnsburg lay—the poet puts in one of the clearest hints at Hrothulf's subsequent treachery: 'þā gȳt wæs hiera sib ætgædere'.[2] As to Wealhtheow's speech, asking Beowulf 'to act as protector of her sons',[3] it ends with the well-known hymn on the loyalty and harmony reigning among the Danes which, in view of the poet's intimations of Hrothulf's treachery (and probable usurpation) may be considered as a fine piece of dramatic irony.[4] Be it as it may, the allusion to the future tragedy of the Danish royal house is clear enough and its effect is obviously heightened by its double contrast with the brilliant scene of splendour and rejoicings in the Hall, and with the glorious Danish victory over their enemies at Finnsburg.

into negotiations with Hengest out of dire military necessity—an explanation which one can hardly credit to the full, since the statement that he had lost all but a few of his thanes is obviously an exaggeration for the sake of increasing the prestige of Hengest and the little Danish band' (K. Malone, *op. cit.*, pp. 163–164). This exaggeration is probably due to the circumstances as much as to the poet's sympathy for the Danes. See the following note.

[1] As Professor Lawrence made clear, 'the circumstances under which the minstrel sang his lay in Hrothgar's hall are important for an interpretation of the story. The subject was selected with a view to giving pleasure to the feasting Danish warriors, celebrating the triumph of a foreign hero, who had performed a feat that they had themselves striven in vain to accomplish. This might well be a little galling to them . . . So the court poet adroitly selected a tale of Danish heroism and Danish vengeance, a tale of the complete and satisfying victory of the Danes over their ancient enemies, the Frisians' (Lawrence, *Beowulf and Epic Tradition*, pp. 109–110). This immediate motivation of the introduction of the Finn story and its character into the poem remains quite true even if we admit, with Professor Malone, that behind the 'happy ending' the tragic note is still there. The assumption that Hengest himself 'never took vengeance', in spite of his longings, and that this knowledge on the part of the audience constitutes a piece of dramatic irony casting 'a pathetic shadow over the vengeance scene' (Malone, *op. cit.*, pp. 169–70), is quite plausible, and would be in the manner of the *Beowulf* poet. It is, however, purely hypothetical, whereas the contrast between the Danish triumph—crushing enough even in the case of Hengest's possible frustration—closing the Episode and the dark implications of the following scene (to which we refer below) finds a real support in the text.

[2] *Beowulf*, l. 1164.
[3] Klaeber, *Beowulf*, p. 179.   [4] See above, p. 31, note 3.

The link with the *Episode*, moreover, transcends this element of contrast, and Professor Lawrence wonders whether it may not be 'that the story of Queen Hildeburh was here designedly brought into connection with the tragedy in store for Queen Wealhtheow, which must have been well-known to the people for whom the poet of *Beowulf* wrote?'[1] Asking the question is already solving it; the parallel between Hildeburh and Wealhtheow is unmistakable. Yet a further link of the greatest importance is to be stressed which makes of that parallel the actual *trait d'union* between the Finnsburg and the Heathobards episodes.

'The telling of the story of Hildeburh', writes Professor Lawrence, 'in the presence of a queen who was herself of another people than that of her husband, whose efforts to keep the peace were destined to come to naught, and whose daughter Freawaru was to experience much the same melancholy destiny as the wife of King Finn, is surely not without significance.'[2] The Wealhtheow scene is thus, in a way, the link connecting—in their striking analogy—the situation of Hildeburh in the Finnsburg Episode, and that of Wealhtheow's daughter Freawaru in the Heathobards Episode. Even if it is not quite certain (though extremely probable) that Hildeburh was likewise used as 'freoðu-webbe' the similarity is obvious enough.

Now the point which is for us of the greatest interest is that the Heathobards Episode is thus not only definitely linked with the Finnsburg Episode but the central theme of both episodes is exactly the same: Beowulf's prophecy concerning Freawaru is in fact but another effective illustration of the theme of the precarious peace.[3] Ingeld's tragic dilemma is almost the exact counterpart of Hengest's, and in both cases the aspect of the sword ('billa sēlest' in the Finnsburg Episode, 'dȳre īren' in the Heathobards Episode),[4] meant the decisive 'call to action' resulting in the victory of the urge for revenge and the outbreak

---

[1] Lawrence, *Beowulf and Epic Tradition*, p. 126.
[2] *Ibid.*, p. 127.
[3] We here refer to Beowulf's 'prophecy', but whether the passage is considered as partly prophetic only (Malone) or as an instance of the use of the 'historical present' (Olrik) is immaterial for us: the main effect of the tragedy is practically the same. We may safely adopt Malone's attitude, who 'did not see that it made much difference, in interpreting the episode, whether the events were thought of as having occurred before or after Beowulf's visit to the Danish court' (K. Malone, 'Time and Place in the Ingeld Episode of "Beowulf",' *Journal of English and Germanic Philology*, XXXIX, Jan. 1940, p. 77; for Malone's interpretation of the episode, see *ibid.*, p. 87).
[4] See respectively ll. 1144 and 2050.

of fresh hostilities. We said 'almost', because, if compared with
the situation of Hengest, Ingeld's represents an even greater
concentration of the dramatic element: not only does the claim
of vengeance force him to break the compact with the former
enemy, as in Hengest's case, but he is now connected by the
bonds of marriage with Freawaru, the Danish princess, and such
bonds render the dilemma even more tragic. It is, to a certain
extent, as if Hengest had been married to a Frisian princess,
say a daughter of Finn! And yet vengeance triumphs, again
emphasizing how fateful indeed was a renewal of the enmity
between the two tribes.[1] It should not be forgotten, moreover,
that the dramatic effect is again heightened by the very similar
contrast wrought between present harmony (the fine picture of
Freawaru amid the rejoicing guests in the Hall), and future
calamity.

Now only are we in a position to interpret the actual value
of the *leitmotiv* of the precarious peace, common to both episodes,
in connection with the organic structure of the poem. In a word
we suggest that this element is to the background of the Danish
part what the impending renewal of the Swedish-Geatish feud
is to that of the Dragon part. Yet it is at the same time no less
than a subtle preparation for that theme that looms so large in the
background of the Dragon part, and gradually imposes itself
in an admirable and oppressive crescendo.

If the episodes that deal with the former Swedish-Geatish
feud are in fact inexorably leading to the great epic prophecy of
the downfall of the Geatish people; if that downfall itself is a
consequence of the inevitable renewal of the feud between the
two nations, then the theme of the precarious peace, as illustrated
in the background of Danish history, already strikes the first
notes of the whole tragedy. After the vivid precedents of the
Finnsburg and Heathobards stories, which are indeed its best
warrant, the outbreak of the war between Swedes and Geats
is felt to be all the more inescapable. The recurrent pictures of
the former fights between the two hostile peoples—especially

---

[1] As a critic writes in reference to Beowulf's prophecy about Freawaru, 'implicit in the
whole story is the strain so dear to the poet of *Beowulf*, fatal inevitability (in the reader's
knowledge) against which human bravery will struggle till the end which is fixed and even
so contested' (B. F. Huppé, 'A Reconsideration of the Ingeld Passage in "Beowulf",'
Journal of English and Germanic Philology, XXXVIII, April 1939, p. 225). It should be added
that the motive of the feud is not only emphasized by Ingeld's spiritual conflict but also by
the 'stern old warrior who will not let the feud die down' (Chambers, *Introduction*, p. 22).

when involving the 'fall of a prince'[1]—are so many milestones leading to the inevitable conclusion: the renewal of the feud is bound to come. And when it is actually prophesied, the ground and atmosphere have been so admirably prepared that it acquires indeed a tremendous power—one shudders at the presence of such implacable doom.

In conclusion we may point out that if Beowulf's personality and actions represent the main thread which runs through the two parts of the poem, the theme that connects these episodes with the background of the Dragon part may be considered as a parallel and corresponding thread—both uniting the Grendel and the Dragon parts in a closer web. This is no mean artistic achievement on the part of the *Beowulf* poet.

---

[1] As in the case with Hrethric and Ongentheow. Compare with the fall of Hnæf in *Finnsburg* and Beowulf's allusion to swords seldom resting after 'hæleða hryre' in connection with the Ingeld episode.

THE monster was angered by the sound of the harp in the hall where the scop was singing:

'Sægde sē þe cūþe
frumsceaft fīra feorran reccan,
cwæð þæt se Ælmihtiga eorðan worh(te),
wlitebeorhtne wang, swā wæter bebūgeð,
gesette sigehrēþig sunnan ond mōnan
lēoman tō lēohte landbūendum,
ond gefrætwade foldan scēatas
leomum ond lēafum, līf ēac gescēop
cynna gehwylcum þāra ðe cwice hwyrfaþ.'

(90–98)

The monster was called Grendel; he was living in the marches

'siþðan him Scyppend forscrifen hæfde
in Cāines cynne—þone cwealm gewræc
ēce Drihten, þæs þe hē Ābel slōg;
ne gefeah hē þǣre fæhðe, ac hē hine feor forwræc,
Metod for þȳ māne mancynne fram.
þanon untȳdras ealle onwōcon,
eotenas ond ylfe ond orcnēas,
swylce gīgantas, þā wið Gode wunnon
lange þrāge; hē him ðæs lēan forgeald.'

(106–114)

The monster's dam had to live in

'cealde strēamas, siþðan Cāin wearð
tō ecgbanan āngan brēþer,
fæderenmǣge; hē þā fāg gewāt,
morþre gemearcod mandrēam flēon,
wēsten warode. þanon wōc fela
geōsceaftgāsta.'

(1261–1266)

Owing to their Christian element and the particular place which should be attributed to them in the poem, the Song of Creation as well as the allusions to the Giants' war against God and to Cain are of especial interest.

The Song of Creation, which, of course, brings into mind Caedmon's Hymn, though it has no other connection with it than the subject-matter, goes back to the Biblical account in Genesis. Whether its introduction has been suggested by the corresponding passage of the *Æneid*[1] (though the frequency of the theme in Anglo-Saxon poetry does not make it necessary to reach as far back) is almost immaterial to us: its immediate artistic design is clear enough. Once more, as has been rightly pointed out by Klaeber, it is a matter of contrast. 'The rare note of joy in the beauty of nature contrasts impressively with the melancholy inspired by the dreary, sombre abode of Grendel.'[2] Professor Tolkien, moreover, thinks it particularly felicitous that it was sung with the harp which aroused the monster's anger: 'so excellent is this choice as the theme of the harp that maddened Grendel lurking joyless in the dark without that it matters little whether this is anachronistic or not.'[3]

Here we enter upon a new element which is of the greatest importance for an appreciation of the further Biblical allusions, and more generally the Christian element in *Beowulf*. The opposition between the pagan background of *Beowulf* and that Christian element (or, viewed from another standpoint, the blending of both elements in the poem) has been repeatedly pointed out, and there is no need to discuss here the different opinions as to their relative significance. Limiting ourselves to the allusions to Cain and the 'Gigantas', we shall see that Professor Tolkien's interpretation seems to us the best and artistically the most satisfactory. Referring to the process by which the monsters of heathen times became, as enemies to mankind, images of the evil spirit, and to the fact that the defeat of the heroes in this temporal world, though poignant, ceased to appear final in view of the possibilities of an eternal victory in the next world, Professor Tolkien thinks that the 'shift is not complete in *Beowulf*.'[4] The Giants (Grendel's kin) regarded as the descendants of Cain are thus 'directly connected with Scripture, yet they cannot be dissociated from the creatures of northern myth, the ever-watchful foes of the gods (and men). The undoubtedly scriptural Cain is connected with *eotenas* and *ylfe* . . . But this is not due to mere confusion—it is rather an indication of the precise point at which an imagination, pondering old and new, was kindled. At this point new Scripture and old tradition touched and

[1] Klaeber, *Beowulf*, p. 131. See also Hoops, *Kommentar*, p. 27.   [2] Klaeber, *ibid.*
[3] Tolkien, *Beowulf, the Monsters and the Critics*, pp. 27–28.   [4] *Ibid.*, p. 23.

ignited. It is for this reason that these elements of Scripture alone appear in a poem dealing of design with the noble pagan of old days. For they are precisely the elements which bear upon this theme. Man alien in a hostile world, engaged in a struggle which he cannot win while the world lasts, is assured that his foes are the foes also of Dryhten.'[1] The demonstration that far from being the result of a mere confusion the introduction of Scriptural elements corresponded in fact to a perfectly conscious artistic design (used as they are in so far as they bear on an essential theme in the poem) is for us particularly valuable.[2]

The poet's achievement is all the more remarkable that these few allusions were enough to convey so pregnant a significance. Yet if they are few, and very brief, they have been most skilfully incorporated with the poem. The first one, naturally enough, in connection with the very introduction of Grendel and the first mention of his attack; the second one, in close correspondence, with the coming into play of Grendel's mother. The third is more indirect yet acquires retrospectively an almost symbolic value which emphasizes the significance of the preceding allusions. The destruction of the 'Gigantas' is said to be carved on the hilt of the magic sword[3] which enabled Beowulf to be saved *in extremis* from the fearful grip of Grendel's mother and deal the monster the fatal blow. Now there is on the one hand a certain dramatic irony in the fact that the monster is finally overcome by the very weapon said to have been wrought by its own ancestors ('ealdsweord eotenisc').[4] On the other hand Beowulf's fight is now definitely felt to partake of the more general struggle between the powers of good and evil as symbolized in the picture of God's destruction of the giants. We were already told that both monsters were of the same kind as the giants: but now we know that God himself actually helped the hero in the most critical part of the fight by directing his attention to the magic sword, the hilt of which precisely depicted God's own direct action against the accursed race. It is almost as if Beowulf had been raised to the rank of God's own champion. God's intervention at this moment of Beowulf's fight is indeed of significance. This is stressed moreover, indirectly, by the fact

---

[1] *Ibid.*, p. 27.
[2] As Professor Tolkien, whom we cannot but quote again, puts it, we have in the poem 'not confusion, a half-hearted or a muddled business, but a fusion that has occurred *at a given point* of contact between old and new, a product of thought and deep emotion' (*op. cit.*, p. 20).   [3] *Beowulf*, ll. 1687–1691.   [4] *Ibid.*, l. 1558.

that it seems particular to the *Beowulf* version of the tale. As Klaeber pointed out: 'in our poem it is God who directs the hero to the victorious sword, whereas in numerous folk-tale versions this rôle falls to the persons (generally women) found in the lower regions where the fight takes place.'[1] It should be added, furthermore, that as trophies of his victory Beowulf brings back both Grendel's head and the hilt of the magic sword.

[1] Klaeber, *Beowulf*, p. 187. On that feature of the Dragon fight, see especially Chambers, *Introduction*, pp. 467–468.

V. THE ELEGY OF THE LAST SURVIVOR
(2247–2266)

THE poet tells us of the origin of the Dragon's hoard. The lone survivor of a noble race has just hidden the treasure (he inherited from his father) in a mound, close to the shore, and exclaims:

'Heald þū nū, hrūse, nū hæleð ne mōstan,
eorla æhte! Hwæt, hyt ǣr on ðē
gōde begēaton; gūðdēað fornam,
feorhbealo frēcne fȳra gehwylcne
lēoda mīnra þāra ðe þis [līf] ofgeaf,
gesāwon seledrēam. Nāh, hwā sweord wege
oððe fe(o)r(mie) fǣted wǣge,
dryncfæt dēore; dug(uð) ellor s[c]ēoc.
Sceal se hearda helm (hyr)stedgolde,
fǣtum befeallen; feormynd swefað,
þā ðe beadogrīman bȳwan sceoldon;
gē swylce sēo herepād, sīo æt hilde gebād
ofer borda gebræc bite īrena,
brosnað æfter beorne. Ne mæg byrnan hring
æfter wīgfruman wīde fēran,
hæleðum be healfe. Næs hearpan wyn,
gomen glēobēames, nē gōd hafoc
geond sæl swingeð, nē se swifta mearh
burhstede bēateð. Bealocwealm hafað
fela feorhcynna forð onsended!'

(2247–2266)

The digression known as the 'Elegy of the Last Survivor' has often been compared with the 'Father's Lament'. Both are fine samples of Anglo-Saxon elegies and are truly typical digressions. Yet, if they have no immediate connection whatsoever with the main story, they play no mean part in the poem owing to the mood in which they are steeped. What we have said, therefore, concerning the 'Father's Lament' holds good as well in the case of the 'Elegy', which can also be said to 'prepare the central theme and dominant mood of the end of the poem.'[1]

Though their action is quite parallel and converging, they

---

[1] See above, p. 34.

have each its own specific ways. The 'Father's Lament', we have seen, as brought about by the Herebeald story, emphasized the inexorability of 'wyrd', the importance of which cannot be over-estimated in the poem. The 'Elegy', on the other hand, as connected with the former story of the hoard, contains an element of anticipation, latent, of course, but artistically of great value. The story of the destruction of a people and the lament of the wretched man who survived the catastrophe fore-shadow the very situation in store for the Geats after Beowulf's death. Both mood and theme are at work here and can be paralleled in the very picture of desolation at the end of the messenger's prophetic speech. The link is significant and again proves how an apparently purely digressional matter can be given a specific action in the organic structure of the poem and even contribute to its unity.

CONCLUSION

As we have concentrated our investigation on the episodes, the main theme of *Beowulf* has generally been suffered to remain 'in the rear'. We therefore think it necessary to point out that we adopt Professor Tolkien's views concerning the general structure of *Beowulf*. The poem 'is essentially a balance, an opposition of ends and beginnings. In its simplest terms it is a contrasted description of two moments in a great life, rising and setting; an elaboration of the ancient and intensely moving contrast between youth and age, first achievement and final death.'[1] Professor Tolkien admirably shows in fact 'the universal significance which is given to the fortunes' of the hero. Viewed in that light the main theme is endowed with a symbolic value and an interest transcending even the most absorbing 'historical' matters which have therefore been subordinated to it and put 'on the outer edges or in the background' to give 'a sense of perspective'.[2] This must be kept in mind now that we are going to draw our conclusions on the artistic interest, not only of the 'historical', but of all the episodes in the poem.

Generally speaking, then, the main advantages which the poem owes to the introduction of so many various episodes are the

---

[1] Tolkien, *op. cit.*, p. 29.

[2] 'It glimpses the cosmic and moves with the thought of all men concerning the fate of human life and efforts; it stands amid but above the petty wars of princes, and surpasses the dates and limits of historical periods, however important. At the beginning and during its process, and most of all at the end, we look down as if from a visionary height upon the house of man in the valley of the world' (*ibid.*, p. 35).
Professor Tolkien's interpretation seems to us indeed by far the most satisfactory dramatically as well as artistically. It is, at the same time, perfectly objective: it considerably heightens our appreciation of the poem by showing the grand simplicity of its original design, its real perspective, its structural force and permanent human element—and all this on a quite solid basis, all the more solid that it is devoid of the speculative element inherent in so many other tentative explanations. It is therefore more convincing than any of those which have been attempted so far, making of the Dragon fight, for instance, either an 'allegorical representation of the fall of the Geats' (Strömholm), or a materialization of an internal discord, or civil war, sapping the national strength of the Geats (Du Bois)—not to speak of the now long since discarded mythological interpretations with which those explanations have, after all, a common element of speculation. When Mr. Du Bois writes, for instance, that 'early audiences would have seen that ideas were represented by these fabulous beings' (*op. cit.*, p. 391), this may be quite right; but whether those beings suggested to early audiences precisely the ideas which the critic sees behind the monsters is another question—there's the rub, just as in the case of the mythological explanations which were finally condemned by the very fact that too many fanciful ideas could be (and actually were) imagined as representing 'the only true and original' mythical explanation of Beowulf and the monsters. It is only fair to add that, however one may dissent from Mr. Du Bois's ingenious and elaborate theory of the monsters, his conclusions that 'the poet was an artist rather than a story-teller, an historian, or a philosopher' (p. 405), and his conception of *Beowulf* as 'pageant-drama' (p. 403) seem quite pertinent.

following. First, the very number and variety of the episodes renders the background of the poem extraordinarily alive; they maintain a constant interest and curiosity in the setting and, by keeping continuously in touch with 'historical' events, represent the realistic note serving as a highly appropriate foil to the transcendental interest of the main theme with its highly significant symbolic value. The way in which many digressions are presented, the allusive manner that so often suggests rather than describes, the light and subtle undercurrent of implications and connotations that runs beneath the vivid pageantry of many scenes, all contribute to create that 'impression of depth' which, as pointed out by Professor Tolkien, justifies the use of episodes and makes them so appealing.[1]

Now by what means did the poet manage, or at least attempt, to avoid the dangers and drawbacks that the use of so many various digressions was almost inevitably bound to carry with it? The most obvious of these drawbacks and the most difficult to overcome was that such an extensive use might have endangered the organic unity of the poem and created an impression of confusion highly detrimental to its artistic value. That many critics have been tempted to think that such was actually the effect of the episodes on the poem, or that some of them were not relevant, perhaps even interpolations, is proof enough of the reality of such a danger. We suggest—and our main object was to make it clear—that the poet actually succeeded to a very large extent in overcoming that danger; and this precisely owing to his artistic sense.

In the first place he was careful to create a number of various links between the different episodes and some aspect of the main story, or between two or more convergent episodes so grouped as to achieve an artistic effect which has a bearing on the main theme; in the latter case each particular episode of the group often happens to have also its own links with its immediate context. These links are extremely varied, some of them very obvious and direct, others much more subtle and implicit—but, however differing in degree, they are all so many links of relevance that

---

[1] See also the following justification: 'Far-flung tales and allusions, apparently scattered material and disconnected events are grouped in a wide sweep around the hero's character. In fact these *are* his character, and their significance in the poem consists in this particular relation; by comparison we are shown Beowulf's nature, by searchlights into the past and future we are to sense the magnitude and true import of his achievements. From this periphery he draws his substance and reality' (Blomfield, *op. cit.*, p. 396).

weave the main theme and its highly dramatic and diversified
background into an elaborate and impressive tapestry.[1]

Most of these links are made tangible by the constant use of
parallelism and contrast. Such a repeated use of the element
of contrast (to take but the favourite device of the poet) almost
systematically applied, might easily have resulted in an appearance of artificiality and rigid symmetry. Yet, precisely because
the very number and diversity of the episodes allowed so many
variations in the use of the device, that danger was avoided too.
Thus the use of contrast, which is at the basis of so many of the
connecting links, thereby contributes to avoid the confusion
such a number and variety of digressions might have created;
and reciprocally the very number and diversity of digressions,
by permitting frequent variations in the use of contrast prevented
its appearing as an automatic device suggesting an impression of
sheer artificiality. There we have, indeed, a hint of the poet's
artistic sense.

Even in episodes where no such links of relevance seem to be
visible we have a particular atmosphere that merges at a given
point in the general mood and contributes to its intended effect.
Consequently we shall draw the important conclusion that
behind all the episodes is found a definite artistic design, clear
enough to allow us to say that each one plays a useful part—
however minute or important—in the composition of the poem.[2]

If we want to classify the digressions according to their
respective rôles—and no longer as we have provisionally done
according to their subject-matter, because it was simply convenient on commencing our study—we meet a difficulty owing
to the fact that most of the digressions have actually more than
one part to play. Yet, without aiming at completeness or, to put
it in Professor Tolkien's expressive way, looking rather to the
strategy and neglecting the minor tactics, we shall attempt a brief
and schematical summary which, though imperfect, may be
useful at least.

It will be convenient to distinguish two great divisions: in
the one we shall class those episodes that concern, above all, the

[1] What Miss Bartlett (from whom we borrow the 'tapestry' simile) writes of the verse
pattern in Anglo-Saxon epic can indeed be applied *mutatis mutandis* to the digressions in
Beowulf (Bartlett, *op. cit.*, p. 7); the change consisting mainly in the suppression of the
restrictive words.
[2] This shows in a striking way how the *Beowulf* poet was intent upon working out what
Miss Bartlett called 'the spaces, the panels, between the pictures' (*op. cit.*, p. 109), as well as
the pictures themselves.

background of the poem: to the other belong the episodes directly connected with the main theme.

I. Here we have the group of four successive episodes dealing with the *Swedish-Geatish Wars*. Each one has its own immediate object, and yet the ultimate purpose of those digressions can only be fully understood if they are considered as a group. Following one upon another (in a succession unparalleled in the poem), they bring home to the audience the theme of the Swedish-Geatish enmity in an impressive gradation. The recurrence of the theme subtly conveys the impression of an impending doom, and leads to the epic prophecy of the downfall of the Geats after Beowulf's death. The dramatic effect of that prophecy is thus considerably heightened.

Indirectly linked with these are—in the first part of the poem— the *Finn* and *Heathobards Episodes*. By illustrating the inexorability of 'wyrd' and the powerful urge for revenge in two rival tribes, both episodes, which have in common the theme of the precarious peace, serve as foreshadowing parallels to the Swedish-Geatish enmity and help to give it its full force. Thereby they prepare the way for that dramatic aspect which gives the background of the poem its portentous significance and finds its climax in the great epic prophecy.

The two *Elegies* finally, by their striking atmosphere of gloom and sadness, help to prepare, and effectively contribute to, the predominantly sombre and oppressive mood in which this climax, and more generally the end of the poem, is steeped. The Elegy of the Last Survivor, moreover, gives us an ominous and subtle premonition of the catastrophe in store for the Geats, so vividly suggested and almost materialized by the great picture of desolation closing the messenger's speech.

Carried to such a degree of dramatic force, this background is certainly the fittest and most effective for the main story; it echoes the great motive of which that story is likewise— though on a universal plane—the fine illustration: 'lîf is lǣne'.[1]

II. We may put the following digressions in a first group: the *Youthful Adventures of Beowulf*, the *Unferth Intermezzo* and *Beowulf in Friesland*. Their principal purpose is to contribute to the presentation and to our better knowledge of the hero by stressing some of his characteristic traits. Some are physical traits such as his fabulous strength and endurance which are to

---

[1] See Tolkien, *op. cit.*, p. 18.

give us confidence in the success of his great undertaking. Others are psychological, such as his courtesy towards the King of Denmark, his keen wit in the dispute with Unferth and his sense of humour, all of which cannot but heighten our esteem of the hero. Besides, the story of the youthful adventures, Unferth's attack and Beowulf's version of the Breca contest are three movements which form a kind of dramatic prologue to the main action. Finally, the psychological situation which motivates the *Ecgtheow digression* incidentally sheds some light on one aspect of the Unferth incident.

A second group consists of the episodes known as *Sigemund and Heremod, Heremod's Tragedy,* together with the last Heremod allusion in conjunction with *Beowulf's Inglorious Youth.* Their object is a glorification of the hero by means of parallels and significant contrasts. The Sigemund and Heremod episode may indeed be considered as a hymn in praise of Beowulf, to which both the scop and the *Beowulf* poet contribute. As to Hrothgar's admonition, which again implies a contrast between Heremod and Beowulf, it is, at the same time—by its subtle anticipation of a new turn in Beowulf's life—a preparation and prologue to the hero's future career. Even the allusion to Beowulf's sluggish youth which emphasizes his prodigious ascent, and the way this ascent is implicitly contrasted to Heremod's disastrous downfall after a few years of great promise, again contribute to the glorification of the hero. One aspect of the *Modthrytho-Offa* digression may, perhaps, allow us to include it in the group.

The short digression on the *Fate of Heorot* and the allusion to the *Brosinga mene* give slight but significant touches representing first minor (and premonitory) variations on a fundamental theme in the poem: the transience of all earthly things, even the most beautiful. A 'vanitas vanitatum' theme illustrated on a larger scale in the course of the poem.

The digressions of the *Biblical Group* show us, and represent, the point of fusion between Northern myth, which gave the poet the frame (or 'accident') of his story, and Christianity, out of which he made the substance.

There only remains the *Scyld Prologue.* Together with the Finnsburg and Heathobards episodes which—though already grouped elsewhere—may, at the same time, be put under this new heading, it forms an artistically important group of episodes contributing to the unity of the poem. As we have shown, they provide significant links between the two main divisions of the poem. In the case of the Scyld Prologue those links consist, on the one hand, in the parallelism between the 'lordless' time from which the Danes suffered before Scyld's advent, and that which is announced at the end of the poem, and, on the other hand, in the symbolic value of both funeral scenes: one that opens the poem and suggests a brilliant future, the other that closes it and represents a glorious past . . . while imminent disaster is looming in the background. The transition between those two main divisions of the poem is furthermore prepared by the Heremod parallel in Hrothgar's sermon, the trend of which shows that the old King addresses and advises Beowulf as a future ruler. Consequently those two closely connected episodes can also be classed within the same group.

This short recapitulation, though encompassing all the digressions which have been dealt with, is far from being exhaustive. Many of the secondary links between the episodes and their context, as well as the more subtle interplay of contrasts and implications underlying some of them, had to be overlooked for clearness' sake: secondary aspects can be found in the study itself.

As has already been intimated, the results of this inquiry now allow us to draw the important conclusion that each digression brings its distinct contribution to the organic structure and the artistic value of the poem. In other words, we have found that all of them, though in different degrees, are artistically justified. If this be admitted, the problem of the relation between the episodic matter and the main narrative is actually solved. As it has been applied, the artistic criterion (which had never been used on a large scale) leads us to suggest that most of the objections against some of the episodes, most of the misgivings as to their relevance to the poem (as well as hints at possible interpolations accounting for their supposed lack of appositeness) can no longer hold—or, to put it less drastically, are rendered for the greater part unnecessary.

The result obtained by the use of the artistic criterion, though it does not amount to an actual proof, thus decidedly points to, and eloquently speaks in favour of, the unity of authorship. Even if it does not exclude other possibilities concerning the genesis of the poem, the subtle and consummate art that underlies the use of digressions in *Beowulf* can best be explained by its unity of authorship.[1] With the poetic power which reached such heights in the treatment of the main story, as interpreted by Professor Tolkien, an interpretation which we hold to be most attractive, can be paralleled the high artistic sense shown in the use of episodes.

Those aspects of the art of *Beowulf* that are revealed in the treatment of its episodes were indeed well worth pointing out. It is for that artistic achievement[2]—part of which we have ventured to explore here—quite as much as for its documentary value that the *Beowulf* poem deserves to survive, and with it the memory of its unknown author: 'Hwæt!'—to use one of his own expressions—'þæt wæs gōd scop'!

[1] Though we have followed a different path we have thus reached the same conclusion as those at which Mr. Batchelor arrived after his study on the style of the poem. 'The comparative regularity of the fall of the curve of variations, and the parallel fall in the number of words found in my vocabulary of compassion, lead me to believe that the *Beowulf* is the work of one composer—not to the opposite view' (Batchelor, *op. cit.*, p. 342). A study of the narrative art of the *Beowulf* poet also led Mr. Haeuschkel to similar conclusions (Haeuschkel, *op. cit.*, p. 97).

Finally, we may add that the technique of characterization, as illustrated by Professor Schücking in the introductive speeches of the Grendel part, shows in an illuminating way how perfectly conscious is that fine aspect of the poet's art. Professor Schücking clearly showed in what way the poet used those speeches as a means of characterizing the speaker himself, and this with the definite purpose of drawing elaborate pictures of ideal types (Wunschbilder). Nay, even less significant characterizing traits than those used in the speeches are of a certain importance, inasmuch as they already 'von der Bewusstheit der dichterischen Technik Zeugnis ablegen' (Schücking, *Heldenstolz*, pp. 30–31). Such conclusions, emphasizing as they do the conscious element of yet another aspect of the poet's art throughout the poem, can also be considered as favouring the assumption of a unity of authorship.

[2] As Professor Tolkien puts it—and after having read his illuminating study one cannot but wholeheartedly approve of this judgment—'There is not much poetry in the world like this' (Tolkien, *op. cit.*, p. 36). At the close of her recent study which, on the structural aspect of *Beowulf*, brings useful complements to Professor Tolkien's demonstration, Miss Blomfield also stresses that 'the writer of *Beowulf* is in fact a true poet; he has created a tragic unity, he sees with the poet's eye which splits and recombines the elements of everyday perceptions' (Blomfield, *op. cit.*, p. 402).

BOOKS QUOTED

Bartlett, A. C.: *The Larger Rhetorical Patterns in Anglo-Saxon Poetry*, New York, 1935.

Batchelor, C. C.: 'The Style of the "Beowulf": A Study of the Composition of the Poem,' *Speculum*, XII, July 1937.

Beaty, J. O.: 'The Echo-Word in "Beowulf" with a Note on the "Finnsburg Fragment",' *Publications of the Modern Language Association of America*, XLIX, June 1934.

Berendsohn, W. A.: *Zur Vorgeschichte des 'Beowulf'*, Kopenhagen, 1935.

Blomfield, J.: 'The Style and Structure of "Beowulf",' *Review of English Studies*, XIV, 1938.

Bonjour, A.: 'The Use of Anticipations in "Beowulf",' *Review of English Studies*, XVI, July 1940.

Bonjour, A.: 'Weohstan's slaying of Eanmund,' *English Studies*, XXVII, February 1946.

Bradley, H.: 'Beowulf,' Article on, *Encyclopædia Britannica*, 11th edition, III.

Chambers, R. W.: *Beowulf, An Introduction*, 2nd edition, Cambridge, 1932.

Du Bois, A. E.: 'The Unity of "Beowulf",' *Publications of the Modern Language Association of America*, XLIX, 1934.

Girvan, R.: *Beowulf and the Seventh Century*, London, 1935.

Haeuschkel, B.: *Die Technik der Erzählung im Beowulfliede*, Breslau, 1904.

Hoops, J.: *Beowulfstudien*, Heidelberg, 1932.

Hoops, J.: *Kommentar zum Beowulf*, Heidelberg, 1932.

Huppé, B. F.: 'A Reconsideration of the Ingeld Passage in "Beowulf",' *Journal of English and Germanic Philology*, XXXVIII, April 1939.

Klaeber, F. (Ed.): *Beowulf and the Fight at Finnsburg*, 3rd edition, New York, 1936 (Supplement, 1940).

Klaeber, F.: 'Unferð's Verhalten im Beowulf,' *Beiblatt zur Anglia*, LIII, 1942.

Lawrence, W. W.: *Beowulf and Epic Tradition*, Cambridge, Mass., 1930.

Malone, K.: 'The Finn Episode in "Beowulf",' *Journal of English and Germanic Philology*, XXV, April 1926.

Malone, K.: 'Young Beowulf,' *Journal of English and Germanic Philology*, XXXVI, January 1937.

Malone, K.: 'Time and Place in the Ingeld Episode of "Beowulf",' *Journal of English and Germanic Philology*, XXXIX, January 1940.

Müllenhoff, K.: 'Die innere Geschichte des Beovulfs,' *Zeitschrift für deutsches Altertum*, XIV, 1869.

Müller, J.: *Das Kulturbild des Beowulfepos*, Göttingen, 1914.

Pons, E.: *Le Thème et le Sentiment de la Nature dans la Poésie Anglo-Saxonne*, Strasbourg, 1925.

Schücking, L. L.: 'Das Königsideal im Beowulf', *Bulletin of the Modern Humanities Research Association*, III, No. 8, October, 1932.

Schücking, L. L.: 'Heldenstolz und Würde im Angelsächsischen,' *Abhandlungen der Philologisch-Historischen Klasse der Sächsischen Akademie der Wissenschaften*, XLII, No. 5, Leipzig, 1933.

Sedgefield, W. J. (Ed.): *Beowulf*, 3rd edition, Manchester, 1935.

Stenton, F. M.: *Anglo-Saxon England*, Oxford, 1943.

Thomas, W.: *Beowulf et les premiers Fragments épiques Anglo-Saxons*, Paris, 1919.

Tolkien, J. R. R.: *Beowulf, the Monsters and the Critics*, London, 1936.

Whitbread, L.: 'Beowulfiana', *Modern Language Review*, XXXVII, October, 1942.

Wülker, R.: *Grundriss zur Geschichte der Angelsächsischen Litteratur*, Leipzig, 1885.

INDEX